The Highly Qualified Teacher

The Highly Qualified Teacher

WHAT IS TEACHER QUALITY AND HOW DO WE MEASURE IT?

Michael Strong

TEACHERS COLLEGE PRESS

Teachers College
Columbia University
New York and London

Published by Teachers College Press, 1234 Amsterdam Avenue, New York, NY 10027

Library of Congress Cataloging-in-Publication Data

Strong, Michael, 1945-
  The highly qualified teacher : what is teacher quality and how do we measure it? / Michael Strong.
       p. cm.
  Includes bibliographical references and index.
  ISBN 978-0-8077-5225-8 (pbk. : alk. paper) — ISBN 978-0-8077-5226-5 (hardcover : alk. paper) 1. Educational accountability—United States. 2. Teacher effectiveness—United States. 3. Academic achievement—United States. I. Title.

  LB3051.S882 2011
  371.102—dc22

                                                              2011015471

  ISBN 978-0-8077-5225-8 (paperback)
  ISBN 978-0-8077-5226-5 (hardcover)

  Printed on acid-free paper
  Manufactured in the United States of America

  18 17 16 15 14 13 12 11   8 7 6 5 4 3 2 1

For Jeanie

Contents

Preface   ix

1. The Occupation of Teaching   1
    Demographics   1
    Salaries   3
    Prestige   4
    Job Satisfaction   6
    Policy Reforms   7

2. What Do We Mean by Teacher Quality?   12
    Teacher Qualifications   12
    Personal Attributes   13
    Pedagogical Skills and Practices   16
    Teacher Effectiveness   16

3. Teacher Quality Research   18
    Teacher Qualifications   18
    Personal Attributes   35
    Pedagogical Practice   40
    Teacher Effectiveness   46
    Teacher Quality Research—
        Assessing the Evidence   48

4. Measuring Teacher Quality   52

Classroom Observation   53
Evaluations by School Administrators   69
Teacher Portfolios   72
Teaching Artifacts   73
Teacher Self-Reports   75
Student Ratings   78
Value-Added Modeling   78
Measuring Teacher Quality—
    Assessing the Evidence   83

5. Experiments in the Identification of Successful Teachers   85

Cognitive Operations   88
The Experiments   90
Implications   102

6. Conclusion: Implications from the Evidence   104

Notes   107

References   123

Index   143

About the Author   156

Preface

My goal for this book is to provide a review of the research and issues related to teacher quality and teacher effectiveness and describe my own project to develop a new measure for evaluating teachers through observation.

In the year 2010 we saw considerable public attention paid to the effectiveness of teachers, specifically regarding their role in raising student achievement levels. Michelle Rhee made waves by instituting new methods for evaluating teachers in Washington, D.C., before resigning after her mentor, the city's mayor, was voted out of office. The *Los Angeles Times* made waves by publishing the value-added scores of its local teachers. President Obama made waves by hiring an education secretary who set in motion plans for stricter accountability for teacher effectiveness with merit pay and other high-stakes decisions to be linked to effectiveness. In such a climate it is desirable, if not mandatory, to have an unbiased overview of the relevant research so that the political movements can be considered within the context of empirical data and scientific research findings. In presenting the results of my own work, I demonstrate one promising and practical method for identifying more and less effective teachers (as defined by their ability to raise test scores) through classroom observation. It can provide useful information for school administrators to assist in their planning of professional development and in their instructional decision making.

ACKNOWLEDGMENTS

Thanks to the Carnegie Corporation of New York for funding my research; to my colleague John Gargani for his statistical expertise, friendship, and moral support; and to my loyal research assistants Victoria Mata and Laura Lindauer.

The Highly Qualified Teacher

1

The Occupation of Teaching

DEMOGRAPHICS

Imagine you were a woman working in Massachusetts in 1834. As a wage-earner, there is a 50% chance you were in the business of braiding palm-leaf hats or straw bonnets and only a 5% possibility you were a teacher.[1] One hundred years later, with the introduction of formalized K–12 schooling, if you worked outside the home in any of the United States, it is likely you would have been a school teacher, as long as you were unmarried. It is doubtful you were braiding hats. Although in the early 19th century most teachers were men, from the 1930s until today it is women who have dominated the teacher workforce, comprising a fluctuating average around 70% through 1991 and increasing to 80% in 2001.[2] The most recent estimate was calculated by Richard Ingersoll and Lisa Merrill in a review of the *Schools and Staffing Survey* (SASS)[3] databases over 20 years. Their analysis shows an increase in the percentage of teachers who are women from 66% in 1980 to 76% in the 2007–8 school year.[4]

In the 1960s, as a woman with a college degree you probably went into teaching.[5] Upon entering the teaching profession in 1960, you were almost certainly smarter than average. In fact, you were as likely as not to have had an IQ of 130 or higher and to have scored well on standardized exams.[6] You continued to suffer from a poor salary, but you had few professional options, and so teaching was an attractive occupational choice.

Since those days, the demographics of the teaching force have changed. Within 10 years, prospective teachers had plummeted to near the bottom of their college class in both achievement and intelligence tests.[7] Teachers' salaries have risen since the 1960s, but other professions have opened up to women so that the percentage of female college graduates who entered teaching dropped from over 50% in 1960 to 15% in the year 2000.[8] When Marigee Bacolod examined the qualifications of young women entering the teaching profession[9] between 1960 and 1990, she found that, among those who scored in the highest quintile on standardized exams, the fraction that became teachers declined by 21 percentage points over those 30 years,

1

while the fraction that entered other professions increased by 22 percentage points.[10] A similar, but much smaller, decline occurred among Black men, while the numbers for White men showed almost no decline. Figure 1.1, demonstrates the evidence that Bacolod relied upon in her analysis, going back as far as World War II.[11] Bacolod's primary source was the National Longitudinal Surveys of Young Men (NLS-YM), Young Women (NLS_YW), and Youth-79 (NLS_Y79).[12]

In an earlier study, Richard Murnane and his colleagues had determined that college graduates who tested with IQs at 130 or above were about as likely to enter teaching during the 1960s as those with IQs averaging around 100. By 1980, graduates with lower IQ scores were four times more likely to enter teaching than those with the higher scores.[14] A U.S. Department of Education report from 1997 found that the mean SAT (Scholastic Aptitude Test) scores of high school seniors who indicated an intention to major in education while in college were significantly lower than those intending to major in either social sciences, arts and humanities, or physical sciences.[15]

Bacolod was able to explain the reduction in teacher quality, as measured by exam performance, by an equivalent decline in *relative* teacher wages and wage growth. The higher the salaries, the more likely were young women to choose teaching. As the pay declined relative to other professions, so did the ability levels of teachers and teachers in training.

Figure 1.1. Decline in Teacher Quality: Evidence from Standardized Test Scores

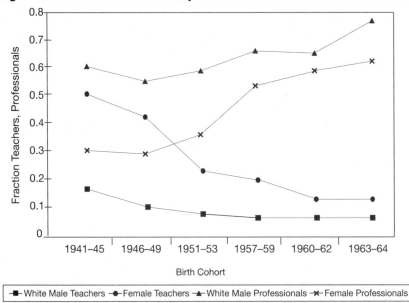

Source: Bacolod, 2007. Sample for this figure includes Black and White respondents with at least 2 years of college. A teacher is a person who taught between age 21 and 30.[13]

Once again, Richard Ingersoll and Lisa Merrill have the latest information on this question.[16] Their analysis of the *Baccalaureate and Beyond Survey* revealed that, in the 1999–2000 academic year, students majoring in education had the lowest average SAT scores, and those majoring in other subjects who went into teaching had lower SAT scores than those who entered other professions. Looking at the quality of the undergraduate institutions attended by teachers, Ingersoll and Merrill found that, in the 2007–8 school year, less than 10% of first-year teachers (but more males than females) had graduated from higher education establishments described as "most" or "highly" competitive by Barron's *Profiles of American Colleges*.[17] In short, however you measure it, the quality of America's teachers appears to be declining.

SALARIES

Several researchers have documented the relative decline in teacher salaries over the second half of the last century, both in Europe and the United States.[18] The economist Darius Lakdawalla describes the decline as a technological change, where the specialized knowledge of skilled workers outside teaching is improved, but not the general knowledge of schoolteachers.[19] Thus, the cost of skilled teachers is raised, but with no equivalent increase in productivity. The response from schools is to lower the relative skill of teachers and raise teacher quantity. The way schools respond cannot be the sole explanation for the decline in teacher quality, however, because the quality of teachers has declined relative to skilled workers in other sectors.[20]

So it is not that teacher real wages failed to grow over the past century. It is just that they didn't increase as much as other professional salaries. The American Federation of Teachers (AFT) conducts an annual survey of teacher salary trends. Its most recent review shows teacher salaries averaging more than $20,000 below the mean for comparative occupations requiring similar education.[21] In 2007, teachers, on average, earned just over $51,000, compared with $63,000 for accountants, $74,000 for architects, and almost $86,000 for computer software engineers. The only occupations from the list of 23 that registered lower salaries than teachers were social workers and athletic trainers. As Michael Podgursky points out, however, there is more to compensation than salary alone.[22] If one takes into account the fact that teachers get summers off and have a shorter workday than many other professionals (although we know many teachers often feel the need to work nights and weekends), and that their fringe benefits including generous retirement packages are also higher than those of many comparable occupations, then the gap is not so great. Podgursky also argues that union reports such as those of the AFT cherry pick the comparison occupations for maximum impact. He suggests using occupations such as journalists, registered nurses, assistant district attorneys, FBI agents, and military officers as more reasonable comparison points.

PRESTIGE

The place of teacher salaries in the rankings is consistent with the prestige or status that people bestow on teaching as an occupation, within a hierarchy of occupations. Occupational prestige has long been the study of sociologists interested in understanding social stratification. They have consistently found a high consensus in prestige ranking among individuals located in different social positions, across different societal contexts, and over time.[23] As far back as 1925, the appropriately named George Counts studied the social status of occupations from the perspective of a vocational counselor, with a particular interest in school teachers. He approached several groups of teachers, university undergraduates, and high school students in different parts of the United States, and asked them to rank 45 occupations "in order of their social standing."[24] He found there to be considerable agreement across the different groups. On the whole, Counts found that the various teaching occupations were given relatively high ranks. He distinguished among college professors (ranked second overall), superintendents (seventh), high school teachers (tenth), elementary school teacher (thirteenth), and rural-school teacher (nineteenth). At the top, in addition to college professors, were bankers, physicians, clergymen, and lawyers. At the bottom were the manual laborers, such as janitors, ditch-diggers, hod-carriers, and waiters.

More recently, the National Opinion Research Center (NORC) conducted a General Social Survey (GSS) that also ranked selected occupations according to their relative prestige. Teaching, like other female-dominated occupations, fell somewhere in the middle, below the top professions of law, academia, and medicine, but above the blue-collar occupations, the police, and secretaries. Within the teaching occupation, secondary school teachers have more prestige than elementary teachers, who, in turn, receive higher status than kindergarten and preschool teachers. Table 1.1 shows the full set of scores for the 1989 rankings from the GSS report.[25]

The data from England are quite similar. A joint study undertaken by researchers from Cambridge University and the University of Leicester examined the status of the "teaching and the teaching profession" in their country.[26] They conducted a number of surveys, including a public opinion survey, a media survey, various teacher surveys, and a survey of teacher recruitment managers. Part of their investigation invited respondents to rate 16 occupations in two ways: 1) as to the current status of the occupation and 2) as to the status that the respondents felt the occupation deserved. Although the occupational categories are fewer and show some differences from the U.S. survey, the general pattern of the results is similar, showing teachers at ranks below the high-prestige professions of medicine and law, and above those of nurses and social workers. Of interest are the opinions regarding deserved status. In this ranking, the legal profession (as represented

**Table 1.1. Relative Prestige of Selected
    Occupations, 1989**

Occupation	Score	Occupation	Score
Physicians	86	Pre-K and kindergarten teachers	55
Lawyers	75	Librarians	54
Professors	74	Funeral directors	49
Physicists/Astronomers	73	Mail carriers	47
Architects	73	Secretaries	46
Chemists	73	Plumbers	45
Chemical engineers	73	Bank tellers	43
Dentists	72	Tailors	42
Aerospace engineers	72	Carpenters	39
Judges	71	Barbers	36
Psychologists	69	Bakers	35
Clergy	69	Painters, construction, maintenance	34
Secondary school teachers	66	Cooks	31
Registered nurses	66	Truck drivers	30
Athletes	65	Cashier	29
Elementary school teachers	64	Waiters and waitresses	28
Authors	63	Garbage collectors	28
Police	60	Janitors/Cleaners	22
Actors and directors	58	Maids	20

Source: Ingersoll & Perda, 2008

in England by barristers and solicitors) falls below both secondary and primary teachers, who are ranked in the same relative order as in the United States. Nurses are also considered worthy of higher status. The full results of this evaluation are shown in Table 1.2.

The English researchers explained the reduced prestige of teaching not only by lower salaries. They suggested that:

if the working conditions and non-financial benefits of teaching could be improved, if external control and regulation was relaxed, and if teaching were seen as a respected and valued authority, part of the gap between the perceptions of a high status profession and the teaching profession would close.[27]

JOB SATISFACTION

However, a study of job satisfaction in the United States casts some doubt on the above opinion. Although lower salaries, a prestige level below that of the more established professions, and often challenging working conditions may influence perceptions about the status of teaching, one may be surprised to find that it ranks among the top 10 for job satisfaction out of 198 occupations.[28] Job satisfaction is an important measure because it is associated closely with overall well-being:

Table 1.2. Ranks of 16 Occupations in England According to Status Currently Held and Deserved

Rank	Current Status	Rank	Deserved Status
1	Surgeons	1	Surgeons
2	Barristers	2	Doctors
3	Doctors	3	Secondary Headteachers
4	Solicitors	4	Primary Headteachers
5	Vets	5	Nurses
6	Accountants	6	Secondary Teachers
7	Management Consultants	7	Primary Teachers
8	Secondary Headteachers	8	Police Officers
9	Web Designers	9	Barristers
10	Primary Headteachers	10	Vets
11	Police Officers	11	Solicitors
12	Secondary Teachers	12	Social Workers
13	Nurses	13	Accountants
14	Primary Teachers	14	Librarians
15	Social Workers	15	Management Consultants
16	Librarians	16	Web Designers

Source: Hargreaves et al., 2006

happy in your job, happy in life. The dozen occupations receiving the highest satisfaction ratings from Tom Smith's 2007 survey are shown in Table 1.3.

At the bottom of the satisfaction scale are mostly unskilled manual and service occupations such as gas station attendants, roofers, and low-level construction workers. On the general happiness scale, teachers dropped from the top 12, whereas special education teachers ranked fifth. It is interesting that prestige ratings are not that closely related either to job satisfaction or general happiness. Physicians and lawyers are absent from the highest group for either scale, although both groups do score above average in satisfaction and happiness. The top 12 list on general happiness can be seen in Table 1.4. Only clergy, firefighters, and special education teachers made the top 12 on both job satisfaction and general happiness. The bottom occupations in general happiness consisted of manual and service occupations.

POLICY REFORMS

In spite of the declining quality of teachers, their relatively low rates of pay, and their mediocre rankings on the prestige list, teachers tend to have high job satisfaction, and there is considerable research to suggest that teacher quality is the single

Table 1.3. Rank Order of Top 12 Occupations in Job Satisfaction

Rank	Occupation
1	Clergy
2	Physical Therapists
3	Firefighters
4	Education Administrators
5	Painters, Sculptors
6	Teachers
7	Authors
8	Psychologists
9	Special Education Teachers
10	Operating Engineers
11	Office Supervisors
12	Security & Financial Services Salespersons

Source: The General Social Survey, National Opinion Research Center, University of Chicago (quoted in Smith, 2007)

**Table 1.4. Rank Order of Top 12 Occupations in
General Happiness**

Rank	Occupation
1	Clergy
2	Firefighters
3	Transport Ticket and Reservation Agents
4	Architects
5	Special Education Teachers
6	Actors and Directors
7	Science Technicians
8	Mechanics and Repairers, Misc.
9	Industrial Engineers
10	Airline Pilots and Navigators
11	Hardware/Building Supplies Salesperson
12	Housekeepers and Butlers

Source: The General Social Survey, National Opinion Research
Center, University of Chicago, (Smith, 2007)

most important school variable influencing student achievement.[29] The economist Eric Hanushek has even estimated the economic value of having a higher-
quality teacher, such that a teacher who is significantly above average in effectiveness can generate annual marginal gains of over $400,000 in present value of
student earnings. Expressed another way, replacing the bottom 5% to 8% of teachers with teachers of average effectiveness could move the United States to near
the top of the international math and science rankings.[30] This research counters
the hitherto discredited, but at the time influential, 1966 study *Equality of Educational Opportunity*, by sociologist James Coleman, who suggested that differences
in teachers did not matter much. The vast study sampled 60,000 teachers in grade
6 and up from more than 3,000 schools. Its principal finding was that nearly all of
the variability in how students achieved was attributable to their socioeconomic
background rather than to the schools they attended. Teacher attributes, such as
teachers' scores on a vocabulary test, their own level of education, and their years
of experience, were found to have little relation to the achievement of White students, and some for Black students. Because Coleman's analyses were conducted
on data that had been aggregated to the school level, his findings were distorted.
For example, the average vocabulary score for all teachers in a school was related

to the average test score for all children in a school. Averaging together the effective teachers with the ineffective teachers, and the high-performing students with the low-performing students, precludes the opportunity to see where teacher characteristics might make a difference.[31]

Unlike in the 1960s, schools today have difficulty attracting the best and brightest college graduates. Three distinct policy reforms have been suggested that might conceivably reverse this trend: professionalization, deregulation, and reforms to the pay structure.[32] The professionalization argument postulates that, only with a set of high standards will the qualities of entering teachers be enhanced, and those of experienced teachers be rewarded. Three educational organizations have set out to develop such standards in the United States: the Interstate New Teacher Assessment and Support Consortium (INTASC), the National Council for the Accreditation of Teacher Education (NCATE), and the National Board for Professional Teaching Standards (NBPTS). The first has developed standards for the preparation and licensure of new teachers, the second attends to the accreditation of teacher training programs, and the third has proposed a set of standards for experienced teachers. The professionalization argument relies on the principle that the state can protect the teaching profession from sub-quality entrants by restricting access to those who meet licensure standards. As Chapter 3 shows, however, research fails to confirm a positive relation between licensure and student outcomes,[33] thus undermining the professionalizing argument as a means for improving teacher quality.

It is important to clarify the distinctions that are made in the education literature between *professionalization* and *professionalism*. While the term *professionalization* refers to the attempts to raise the standards of teaching in such a way that it attains the status of *profession* in the eyes of the general public, *professionalism* refers to the manner in which teachers conduct themselves. In the introduction to their book *Teachers' Professional Lives*, Andy Hargreaves and Ivor Goodson define *professionalization* as the "social and political project or mission designed to enhance the interests of an occupational group," and *professionalism* as "something which defines and articulates the quality and character of people's actions within that group."[34]

That the occupation of teaching fits within the parameters of a profession is the subject of vigorous debate, not least because the concept of profession is itself contested. To paraphrase Eric Hoyle, it is not a precise concept but more an evaluative one.[35] The prominent sociologist Amitai Etzioni referred to teaching as one of the *semi*-professions, along with nursing and social work. He used the term *semi-profession* with no intended derogatory implication to distinguish an occupation whose:

> training is shorter . . . less legitimated, their right to privileged communication less established, there is less of a specialized body of knowledge, and they have less autonomy from supervision or societal control than "the" professions.[36]

Andy Hargreaves characterized the changes that have occurred since the 1960s by postulating four ages of professionalism in teaching: the pre-professional age (where teaching was seen as managerially demanding but technically simple), the age of the autonomous professional (where the singularity and unquestioned traditions of teaching were challenged), the (still emerging) age of the collegial professional (where efforts are directed toward building strong professional cultures, responding to reform, efficacy, and individualized professional development), and the post-modern age (marked by "a struggle between forces and groups intent on de-professionalizing the work of teaching, and other forces and groups who are seeking to re-define teacher professionalism and professional learning in more positive and principled postmodern ways that are flexible, wide-ranging and inclusive in nature").[37] It is in such a climate that the struggle for and against the professionalization of teaching continues.

The deregulation argument takes the opposite position to that of the professionalization movement. Proponents of deregulation claim that there are no established standards for teacher practice, and that teachers may acquire their skills through a variety of paths that need not include a traditional teacher training program. This attracts individuals into teaching who may be highly qualified in other ways, but would not have considered teaching if they were required to fulfill the traditional licensure requirements. Organizations such as Teach for America that attract bright individuals from a variety of fields into teaching, with apparently positive results, provide some foundation for this argument.[38] Educators such as Linda Darling-Hammond argue forcefully against deregulation and alternative paths to certification, maintaining that they result in teachers who lack the necessary pedagogical skills to be competent in many settings.[39]

The argument for addressing the decline in teacher quality by substantially raising teacher pay would not only be costly, but would be likely to have minimal effect in the short term. Even if the occupation becomes more attractive to the higher-level college graduates, there is little evidence of any direct connection between teacher pay and student outcomes. Also, it is difficult to structure a satisfactory plan for salary increases. Instituted across the board, salary increases would lead to a decline in job opportunities because fewer teachers would quit and retirements would be postponed. Raising the salaries of new teachers would work only up to the point that they did not exceed the salaries of experienced teachers. The alternative approach of linking monetary rewards to actual classroom performance in the form of merit pay makes more economic sense, but is highly controversial (especially with the teacher unions, which have lobbied against merit pay at national and local levels[40]), and, in some cases, has been shown to have negative effects in schools that have experimented with such an approach.[41] A recent suggestion for using merit pay to improve the quality of teachers in low-performing schools is to qualify teachers with demonstrated records of student achievement as members of America's Teacher Corps, and offering them a large bonus to teach in the more challenging schools.[42]

However, not all educators are averse to merit pay and, like it or not, this is the direction in which the United States may be moving. In 2009, President Obama earmarked more than $4 billion for the identification and cultivation of effective teachers under the slogan *Race to the Top*. Many states have applied for this money, including Washington, D.C., whose Schools Chancellor Michelle Rhee (now resigned), an early advocate of merit pay, was herself a Teach for America teacher. To qualify, states must first facilitate the linking of student test scores to teachers so that value-added measures can be calculated. Successful applicants must also begin distinguishing between effective and ineffective teachers, and to consider that information when deciding whether to grant tenure, give raises, or fire a teacher or principal. Further, states must publish annually which of their education and other preparation programs produced the most effective (and ineffective) teachers and principals. Once again, the teacher unions, particularly the National Education Association (NEA), are in opposition. The NEA Web site raises a number of objections to pay for performance based on student test scores. Here is a relevant quote:

> Such a move comes with serious, potential pitfalls. For example, when pay raises are based on student test scores, you're only measuring a narrow piece of the teacher's work. In addition, such plans can pit employee against employee, especially when there's a quota for merit increases. What happens to teachers who do not teach tested subjects? How are they rewarded?[43]

Agree or not, one cannot ignore the widespread focus on defining and measuring teacher effectiveness, identifying effective teachers, attracting them to the profession, and rewarding them so they remain in the classroom. For the remainder of this book, we will explore what is meant by teacher quality and teacher effectiveness, examine the research on teacher quality, consider how teachers might best be evaluated, and investigate how good and successful teaching relate to one another.

2

What Do We Mean by
Teacher Quality?

In Chapter 1, we saw that researchers have documented the decline in teacher quality and claimed that teacher quality is the most important school influence on student learning. We may, therefore, be excused for assuming that everyone agrees on what is meant by the term *teacher quality*. This assumption could not be more wrong. The term *quality* is inherently value-laden, so that one person's or group's characterization might legitimately differ from another's, with neither one having more or less veracity. Furthermore, the term *quality* is often used synonymously with other terms such as *master* or the adjectives *good* and *effective*, which themselves may have, under certain conditions, specific and narrower definitions.

Characterizations of teacher quality as discussed in the literature vary according the perspectives and interests of the writer. Definitions may be grouped broadly according to whether they focus on the qualifications of the teacher as a reflection of competence (e.g., degree, quality of college, exam scores, certification, subject-matter credential, experience), the personal or psychological qualities of a teacher (such as love of children, honesty, compassion, fairness), the pedagogical standards that a teacher exhibits (use of certain teaching strategies, classroom management skills, establishment of a positive classroom climate), or the teacher's demonstrated ability to raise student learning (successful or effective teaching).

TEACHER QUALIFICATIONS

Part of President Bush's education act of 2001, No Child Left Behind (NCLB), required all states to provide evidence that their schools' classrooms were staffed with *highly qualified* teachers in time for the 2005–6 academic year. It was up to the states to define highly qualified, which they did usually in terms of what Michelle Rhee, a former chancellor of Washington, D.C., Public Schools, calls "front-end qualifications."[1] Typically, the evidence that states provided on their teachers' qualifications was based on their licensure requirements. The interpretation of teacher quality in this context rests on the assumption that teachers with the right kinds of established qualifications will provide high-quality instruction to American children. As David Berliner pointed out, this assumed that the nation's schools were previously employing teachers who were *not* highly qualified. Berliner contests this assumption, maintaining that the call for highly qualified teachers was largely a political ploy to a) scare the public into thinking that American children were being taught by unqualified teachers, and b) to make it seem as if something was being achieved in the furtherance of public education, when, in reality, no serious problem was being addressed.[2] This position attributes a somewhat cynical motivation to the political purposes behind NCLB and of defining teacher quality in this manner, but as Linda Blanton and colleagues have noted: "The role of policy makers at every level—national, state, and local—cannot be underestimated."[3]

PERSONAL ATTRIBUTES

One advantage of defining teacher quality in terms of competence as indicated by qualifications, credentials, or experience is that these variables are objective and relatively easy to measure. A focus on psychological or personal attributes often represents a shift into the realm of subjectivity. For example, in a study conducted toward the middle of the last century, Paul Witty reviewed 12,000 letters from children who had been asked to describe "'the teacher who has helped me most.'"[4] He found that the children consistently mentioned certain characteristics, the top 12 of which were:

1. Cooperative, democratic attitude
2. Kindliness and consideration for the individual
3. Patience
4. Wide interests
5. Personal appearance and pleasing manner
6. Fairness and impartiality
7. Sense of humor
8. Good disposition and consistent behavior
9. Interest in pupils' problems
10. Flexibility
11. Use of recognition and praise
12. Unusual proficiency in teaching a particular subject.

Some of these traits, particularly related to warmth and friendliness, have continued to surface in later studies that examine students' opinions about good teaching; others relate more to teaching practice and fit better into the category of pedagogical standards.[5] All of them rely on subjective impressions.

A more recent study of this nature was conducted by Robert Walker.[6] Over a period of 15 years at several different institutions, he asked his undergraduate and graduate students, many of whom were education professionals returning to school for advanced degrees, to describe the qualities of teachers who had been most effective in helping them learn and achieve success. The 12 most frequently mentioned characteristics in his study were a mix of personal (e.g., friendliness, compassion, sense of humor) and teaching traits (well prepared, having creative teaching methods). Here is the full list:

1. Came to class prepared
2. Maintained positive attitudes about teaching and about students
3. Held high expectations for all students
4. Showed creativity in teaching the class
5. Treated and graded students fairly
6. Displayed a personal, approachable touch with students
7. Cultivated a sense of belonging in the classroom
8. Dealt with student problems compassionately
9. Had a sense of humor and did not take everything seriously
10. Respected students and did not deliberately embarrass them
11. Were forgiving and did not hold grudges
12. Admitted mistakes

Sometimes it is teachers themselves, rather than students, who are polled for their opinions on the characteristics of a quality teacher. Teachers, particularly those who work with younger children, tend to believe that a primary attribute of a good teacher is to be caring and to like or love children.[7] Furthermore, the beliefs of pre-service teachers are well formed before they enter their training programs because of years of experience in the classroom, and they change little over the course of their training programs.[8] Some teacher educators, therefore, see the definition of a good teacher as a combination of personal attributes that have to do with being caring and liking children and with professional attributes related to content and pedagogical knowledge.[9]

Terry Hyland, a British teacher educator wrote vigorously against the move toward competency-based educational strategies because they fail "to capture the essential epistemological and moral dimensions of the work of professionals."[10] Hyland's view is more aligned with the humanistic approach to teacher education that developed out of the humanistic psychology of Abraham Maslow and Carl Rogers in the early 1970s,[11] which focused on personal growth and development of the self.[12] Although humanistic approaches were not widely adopted, we see an emphasis on developing the personal characteristics of teachers in the writings of some British and American educators. These writers refer to the "personal qualities" of a good teacher such as creativity, trust, care, courage, sensitivity, decisiveness, spontaneity, commitment, and flexibility[13], or "core qualities" and "effective personal behavior" to be developed in high-quality teachers through the reflection process.[14]

An interesting twist on the definition of teacher quality representing a perspective that bridges the concepts of competence, personal qualities, and practice comes from the Yale psychologist Robert Sternberg and his colleague Joseph Horvath. They argue for making a distinction between expert and experienced teachers through the psychological understanding of how experts differ from non-experts. They invoke the work of Eleanor Rosch on prototypes to define the prototypical category of "expert."[15] They identify three domains in which expert teachers differ from non-experts: *knowledge* (experts "bring knowledge to bear more effectively" within their areas of expertise); *efficiency* (experts do more in less time within their areas of expertise); and *insight* (experts "are more likely to arrive at novel and appropriate solutions" within their areas of expertise).[16] Their approach is a way of thinking about teacher quality that allows for numerous prototypes, and so for different ways of being a high-quality teacher. In their own words, they claim:

> that by viewing teaching expertise as a prototype, we can distinguish experts from experienced non-experts in a way that acknowledges (a) diversity in the population of expert teachers, and (b) the absence of a set of individually necessary and jointly sufficient features of an expert teacher. Thus, a teacher who displays a wealth of highly organized content knowledge and a teacher who is adept at generating insightful solutions to classroom problems may both be categorized as experts, even though their resemblance to one another is weak.[17]

The ideas of Sternberg and Horvath have potentially useful implications for the evaluation of teachers and teaching, but have not really caught on among educators. By defining expert teaching as representing the prototype characteristics that experienced educators have seen or heard about, Sternberg and Horvath allow for the expectation of systematic differences in the ways that individuals or groups judge teaching expertise. These differences would be a reflection of the observer's differing experience, thus allowing for the prototypical expert behaviors of an elementary teacher to vary from those of middle or high school instructor, and those of a math teacher to differ from those of an English or a music teacher. Sternberg and Horvath emphasize that their approach gets at the concept of teacher quality through a prototype *view* rather than a prototype *model*. In its present form, their view of expert teaching may encourage us to rethink how we conceptualize teacher quality, but does not provide us with a clear way of evaluating a given teacher. In order for this perspective to take hold, it will need to be validated and almost certainly revised. However, this line of thinking offers a new way of approaching the recruitment, training, selection, and assessment of teachers, and has implications for our notions of the necessary and sufficient attributes of an effective teacher.

PEDAGOGICAL SKILLS AND PRACTICES

Those interested in reforming education tend to think of teacher quality solely in terms of classroom practice rather than of the front-end qualifications or personal attributes that a teacher may possess. Several organizations have issued curriculum standards and guidelines that direct reform-minded practice and indicate what constitutes quality teaching from their perspectives.[18] These organizations define quality teachers as conducting instruction that engages students as active participants in their own learning and enhances the development of complex cognitive skills and processes. For mathematics, this view is described most clearly in documents produced by the National Council of Teachers of Mathematics (NCTM), whose vision of mathematics curriculum emphasizes problem-solving, communication, reasoning, and mathematical connections.[19] These four standards are included at every grade level, along with content standards that vary by grade. The proposed curricula reform is accompanied by five major shifts in the nature of classroom instruction.[20] Reform teachers:

1. view classrooms as mathematical communities rather than collections of individuals;
2. use logic and mathematical evidence to verify results rather than relying on the teacher as the authority;
3. emphasize mathematical reasoning rather than memorizing procedures;
4. focus on conjecture, inventing, and problem-solving rather than mechanical answer finding; and
5. make connections among the ideas and applications of mathematics rather than seeing them as isolated concepts and procedures.

These changes in instruction should be evident in the mathematical tasks that teachers select, the roles of teachers and students in mathematical discourse, the tools that are used to enhance classroom discourse, the classroom learning environment, and teachers' analysis of teaching and learning. Although endorsed by the National Science Foundation (NSF) and the U.S. Department of Education, the NCTM standards have been heavily criticized in some corners (a controversy often referred to as "the math wars"), resulting in parental revolts and the formation of some anti-reform organizations that promote memorization of basic skills and facts, and that have succeeded in causing textbooks to be replaced in some parts of the United States.[21]

TEACHER EFFECTIVENESS

The final group of teacher quality definitions refers to effective or successful teaching as measured by student outcome measures. In their analysis of the concept of quality in teaching, Gary Fenstermacher and Virginia Richardson draw attention to the important distinction between *good teaching* (the worthiness of the activity) and *successful teaching* (the realization of intended outcomes), then go on to make the point that *quality teaching* encompasses both good and successful teaching.[22] They conclude that an assessment of quality teaching requires that, in addition to focusing on the teacher, one take into account contextual factors such as the state of the learners, the character of the social surroundings, and the availability and extent of the opportunity to teach and learn. Thus, the nature of teacher quality, to their way of thinking, is elusive and contested, yet there are still those who profess to know how to evaluate it:

> [This] has not stopped others from asserting that they know quality teaching when they see it, they know how to determine whether it is occurring or not, and they know this across schools, districts, states, and nations. Many such claims lack not only a good understanding of teaching but also a humility for the challenge of appraising anything so complex as the nature and consequences of human relationships, particularly between adults and children in the otherwise unworldly setting of the schools of the early 21st century.[23]

We will get to a deeper discussion of the problems of assessing and evaluating quality teaching in Chapter 4. Today, those who view teacher quality as synonymous with effective teaching as defined by student outcomes commonly use a statistical procedure known as value-added modeling (VAM) to assess effectiveness. VAM refers to a collection of statistical techniques that use multiple years of student test-score data to estimate the effects of individual schools or teachers on student achievement.[24]

However, in spite of the widespread attention paid to standardized test scores as a measure of school and teacher effectiveness in the United States, there are other kinds of student outcomes advocated by many parents and educators. These might include increased motivation to learn or love of learning,[25] dropout or graduation rates,[26] participation in advanced courses[27] and college acceptance rates, or other social, behavioral, or intellectual outcomes

Some of these outcomes are often linked to broader notions of school or educational effectiveness as opposed to teacher effectiveness. There is a recent movement in some circles toward generalizing the definition of effectiveness outcomes to include, for example, moral and social value formation, in addition to the cognitive outcomes of the classroom performance of teachers.[28] Also, it is suggested that, rather than attempting to identify a single set of characteristics of teacher effectiveness that apply in all teaching situations, one should adopt a differentiated model that allows for different indicators of effectiveness in different teaching settings. This might include a teacher's work outside the classroom,[29] as well as differences in curriculum or subject matter, grade level, and student socioeconomic or linguistic status.[30] This idea harkens back to the work of Sternberg and Horvath on experts and prototypes, which also offers a differentiated view of high-quality teaching.

3

Teacher Quality Research

Having seen that teacher quality may have a variety of definitions, we can now attend to an assessment of the evidence related to the connection between the different kinds of teacher quality and educational outcomes. We will consider them in the groupings identified in Chapter 2: front-end teacher qualifications, personal attributes, pedagogical practice, and effectiveness. The fourth definition, effectiveness in improving student outcomes, is at once a dependent variable for research on other aspects of teacher quality, and a measure of teacher quality in itself. Therefore, the research on effectiveness serves to demonstrate the contribution of the teacher to student educational outcomes. The purpose of this section is to provide a thorough overview of the main findings of the research on teacher quality, rather than an exhaustive description of every study that examines the link between some form of teacher quality and some representation of student learning. Other researchers have provided syntheses from this research in the recent past, and together constitute a solid resource.[1] The synthesis provided here organizes the studies within the framework I have set up for considering teacher quality, emphasizes the studies that I think are the most important or interesting, and introduces some of the most recent work on this topic that may have appeared since the other syntheses were published. It is only after learning about the research that has been conducted on the different aspects of teacher quality that one is in a position to focus on policy considerations.

TEACHER QUALIFICATIONS

Under this category of teacher quality reside a wide variety of variables. These comprise:

- Certification
- Undergraduate major or minor
- Undergraduate institution

- Advanced degree(s)
- Type of preparation program
- Test scores
- Pedagogical content knowledge
- Level of professional development
- Teaching experience

In general, findings across all these kinds of qualifications are mixed. Sometimes, when an intuitively important qualification appears to have little or no influence on student outcomes, the finding may be influenced by the study's small sample size, insensitive statistical analyses, or imperfect databases. Furthermore, different kinds of qualifications may be important in different teaching settings: urban or rural, high or low poverty, elementary or secondary, science or reading. We should bear these facts in mind when considering the research.

Certification

Most studies comparing certified and uncertified teachers find a positive association between regular certification and student achievement.[2] There have been, however, a couple of notable exceptions. For example, in one study, high school students of mathematics teachers with temporary emergency credentials were found to have achievement profiles no worse than the students of certified teachers.[3] The authors of this study, Dan Goldhaber and Dominic Brewer, speculate that because most of the teachers with emergency certificates were located in high-poverty schools that had difficulty attracting certified teachers, districts were extra careful to screen the uncertified individuals for ability or content knowledge. This suggests that the important factor may be subject-specific knowledge, at least for math, rather than certification in general. This hypothesis holds up in another study published in one of the National Bureau of Economic Research's many working papers, where authors Christopher Jepsen and Steven Rivkin, in an examination of class size reduction in California, found small certification effects on teacher value added to mathematics and reading achievement.[4]

A further study found that elementary students in San Diego achieved greater gains in both reading and math when taught by an emergency-credentialed teacher than students taught by fully credentialed teachers. This did not apply at the middle and high school levels.[5] These counterintuitive findings may also be explained by the fact that the emergency-credentialed teachers may have had stronger-than-average subject-matter knowledge.

These studies fit the common finding from research on the influence of teacher certification on student outcomes that math certification makes a difference, especially at the secondary level, whereas certification in general does not always show an advantage. Back in 1985, Parmalee Hawk and colleagues studied a small sample of 36 6th- to 12th-grade mathematics teachers in North Carolina, half of whom were certified in mathematics and half were teaching out-of-field (i.e., were certified in some other subject). Teachers were paired by school, one from each group teaching the same grade. Pre-tests at the beginning of the year showed no differences between the two groups. End-of-year tests showed significantly higher math scores for the students who had been taught by teachers with math certification.[6] More recently, Linda Cavalluzzo studied high school teachers in Miami-Dade County Public Schools. With a database of more than 100,000 student records she found, among other things, that having a teacher with state certification in mathematics predicted higher achievement scores.[7]

Linda Darling-Hammond, long an advocate of traditional teacher preparation programs, conducted a study with colleagues using data from Houston schools to determine whether certification had an effect on student achievement. They examined 5 years of student data tied to more than 4,000 4- to 5th-grade teachers in order to compare outcomes for students of certified and uncertified teachers. They found that lack of certification resulted in lower achievement gains.[8]

In contrast, Tom Kane and colleagues, in their examination of certification status among New York City teachers, found that certification was less important than other characteristics in determining student outcomes. Their sample consisted of nearly 10,000 elementary and middle school math and reading teachers of three kinds: certified, uncertified, and alternatively certified. They found that differences in student achievement outcomes within groups were greater than those between groups, suggesting that certification status was less reliable as a predictor of teacher effectiveness than subsequent on-the-job performance.[9]

A number of researchers have looked at the effects of advanced certification, specifically whether teachers who attain National Board Certification (NBC)[10] show additional effectiveness with regard to student achievement. For example, in her previously cited study, Linda Cavalluzzo compared the math performance of Miami-Dade students with teachers who had never attempted to obtain NBC against those of teachers who obtained NBC, who attempted and failed, and who attempted and withdrew. She found that students of teachers who attained NBC had greater achievement gains.

Several researchers have examined data from North Carolina. In one of these studies, Dan Goldhaber and Emily Anthony considered whether NBC was a good signal of effective teaching and whether it was a catalyst for good teaching among North Carolina teachers.[11] In other words, were NBC teachers more effective than those who did not apply or failed the test, and did the process of becoming an NBC teacher lead to greater effectiveness? They found that the students of teachers with NBC performed slightly better than the students of non-NBC teachers in both reading (4% of a standard deviation) and math (5% of a standard deviation), differences that have statistical but little practical significance. They tested to see if NBC added information about teacher quality over and above that learned from regular licensure tests and concluded that it did. With their data, which tracked student performance before and after the teachers received NBC, Goldhaber and Anthony were able to test teacher effectiveness pre- and post-certification. Surprisingly, they found that teachers appeared to be more effective before receiving NBC than after. They hypothesized that the efforts in preparing for NBC may lower a teacher's performance during that year, and that subsequently their elevated credential may cause these teachers to be directed into non-classroom responsibilities that also detract from their ability to raise student achievement levels.

A second group of researchers, led by Charles Clotfelter from Duke University, looked at North Carolina data from a longer and more recent time period, and found similar signaling effects for NBC (those teachers who apply for NBC are more effective than teachers who never apply for advanced certification), but did not see the drops in effectiveness that Goldhaber and Anthony observed during the application year. In fact, Clotfelter and colleagues observed increases for the high school teachers in their sample during the application period (Goldhaber and Anthony did not include high school teachers in their sample).[12] Like Goldhaber and Anthony, Clotfelter and colleagues found that NBC elementary teachers are slightly more effective than non-NBC teachers in reading instruction. Their findings in math, however, were different. They reported that elementary school NBC teachers are slightly more effective than non-NBC teachers in math instruction, whereas Goldhaber and Anthony found no significant difference.

What these two sets of studies tell us is that NBC seems to be a reasonable indicator of teacher quality (NBC teachers have slightly higher student gains than non-NBC teachers, although these differences vary according to grade and poverty levels), but may not be a cost-effective method for raising teacher quality, as effectiveness may go down for some teachers during and after the application process.

Yet another group of researchers, commissioned by the National Board for Professional Teaching Standards (NBPTS), also studied the effects of NBC in North Carolina, restricting themselves, however, to a small sample of 307 5th-grade teachers.[13] They first examined whether 5th-grade teachers with NBC (N = 25) were more effective in raising student achievement scores than non-NBC teachers (N = 282). Unlike Goldhaber and Anthony and Clotfelter and colleagues, they found no significant differences. In fact, 20% of the NBC teachers fell into the bottom quartile of all the 5th-grade teachers in their database. In a second step, they then went on to study a subgroup of 51 teachers for outcomes other than student achievement. They did this by comparing the NBC teachers (N = 21) with the most (N = 16) and least (N = 14) effective non-NBC teachers (as determined by value-added scores) on a number of outcome variables. These included self-perceptions of their own efficacy, planning and assessment practices, cognitive demand of student and teacher questions, student behavior and classroom management strategies, quality of reading assignments, and level of teacher effectiveness from classroom observations using a Teacher Effectiveness Rating Form.[14] They found that NBC teachers had slightly more effective planning practices and produced significantly higher ratings on the degree of cognitive challenge of typical assignments compared with non-NBC teachers. No differences were recorded in the cognitive demand of questions or the amount of disruptive student behavior and the kinds of interventions teachers used to control it. Differences were found in classroom management, classroom organization, positive relationships, and the encouragement of responsibility. In all four of these dimensions, the NCB group fell between the upper and lower non-NBC groups. The authors note some deficiencies in the original database as well as small sample size and the restriction to a single grade level as limitations that should preclude one from generalizing much from their study. Their work adds to our knowledge in that they examined various kinds of teaching outcomes, indicating that effectiveness is not apparent systematically across the different observable variables.

In a further study of North Carolina teachers, William Sanders and colleagues also found no differences between NBC and non-NBC teachers.[15] They tested different models in their sample of more than 4,600 teachers (of whom 587 were NBC teachers) to investigate whether student achievement gains were affected by year in school, race, sex, teacher experience, and NBC status. They concluded, as did Tom Kane and colleagues regarding general certification, that the variation in effectiveness among teachers of the same certification status was large enough to drown out any small differences between groups of different NBC status.

The most recent study of NBC teachers was conducted in Florida by Doug Harris and Tim Sass. They had access to a 4-year database of all teachers and students in that state. Their findings showed little evidence for NBC as a signal of effective teaching, except in a few isolated cases. Like those who studied the North Carolina data, they also found that the process of achieving National Board Certification does not increase teacher productivity.[16]

Undergraduate Major or Minor

The academic preparation of teachers is, in no small part, influenced by the courses that future teachers take in college, as indicated by their undergraduate major or minor. Some researchers have looked at this variable, among others, in their studies of teacher quality and teacher effectiveness. David Monk included data on undergraduate major as an indicator of qualifications related to subject-matter knowledge among secondary math and science teachers. Using the National Assessment of Academic Progress (NAEP) database, Monk found that student learning gains in math were not related to a teacher having been a mathematics major, but in science they were.[17] Conversely, Harold Wenglinsky found, in his analysis of more recent NAEP data, that students whose math or science teachers had a major or minor in the relevant subjects were 39% of a grade level ahead of other students in both subjects.[18]

Undergraduate Institution

Another way of characterizing the qualifications of teachers is to categorize them according to the ratings of their undergraduate institutions. Back in 1977, economists Anita Summers[19] and Barbara Wolfe examined data on teachers and students in Philadelphia and found that "teachers who received B.A.s from higher rated colleges were associated with students whose learning rate was greater—and it was students from lower income families who benefitted most."[20] Clotfelter and colleagues included this variable in their study of North Carolina teachers, cited in the previous section. They used *Barron's College Admissions Selector* to construct three levels of institutional competitiveness (uncompetitive, competitive, and very competitive) and unranked. They found an advantage for teachers coming from competitive institutions, but teachers from elite or very competitive universities were no more effective than teachers from other institutions.[21] Ronald Ehrenberg and Dominic Brewer used the *High School and Beyond* longitudinal study dataset[22] and the same institution ratings from *Barron's* to conclude that "students' gain scores are higher when teachers come from more selective institutions."[23] In their study of Chicago public school teachers, Daniel Aaronson and colleagues found that ". . . quality of college attended . . . [was] loosely, if at all . . ." related to estimated teacher quality.[24]

Advanced Degrees

Many of the researchers already cited included a variable for advanced degrees in their analyses. Until recently, close to 40% of K–12 teachers had a master's degree, for which they are usually entitled to an increase in salary. From a fiscal perspective, it is of interest whether this elevation in educational qualifications translates to increases in student learning and is accordingly worth the extra salary investment. As it turns out, findings are inconsistent across the studies that have included advanced degree as a variable. Most often, they report no relationship, but there are many variations on this theme.

Dan Goldhaber and Dominic Brewer, both labor economists, examined data from the National Educational Longitudinal Study of 1988 (NELS:88).[25] In general, they found that 10th-grade mathematics students performed no better when their teachers had master's degrees. However, after disaggregating the data, they found that, when a teacher's advanced degree was in mathematics, those students made greater achievement gains than the students of teachers with no master's degree, or a non-mathematics master's degree. For other subjects such a relationship did not show up.[26] The researchers who examined certification status among San Diego teachers likewise found that elementary teachers with a master's in mathematics contributed marginally more to increased math scores than teachers with only bachelor's degrees.[27] The findings from other researchers ranged from determining that a master's degree actually had a negative effect on student achievement,[28] no effect one way or the other,[29] or a positive effect.

Type of Preparation Program

Another way of looking at a teacher's qualifications is to examine the kinds of preparation teachers receive before they begin work in the classroom. Many studies have investigated the effects of individual programs, others distinguish between traditional and alternative training programs, and still others have examined the components of preparation such as subject matter, pedagogy, and clinical experiences. In this section, we will focus on the studies of traditional and alternative programs.

Traditional preparation programs are those offered by universities and colleges, both large and small, public and private. Programs at these institutions may vary widely in quality, duration, structure, and content. Most alternative programs were introduced in the early 1990s by states to combat the teacher shortages, especially in the fields of math and science, to attract a more diverse teaching force, and to fill vacancies in urban and rural schools. These programs have been characterized as effectively establishing an accelerated path to alternative licensure, whereby the traditional university or college route is bypassed.[30] Teachers from alternative programs should be distinguished from uncertified or emergency-credentialed teachers, who are in the process of studying for a traditional credential while they teach.

Like traditional programs, alternative programs also vary widely in method of recruitment, content, amount of required coursework, structure, and hours of student teaching. They range from those that are university-based to others such as the nonprofit Teach for America, the U.S. government's Troops to Teachers, and New York City's Teaching Fellows programs. The National Center for Alternative Certification (NCAC) reports that, by 2007, all 50 states and the District of Columbia had at least some type of alternative program, offering a total of 130 different routes to certification. By the end of 2006, approximately 59,000 individuals had been issued teaching certificates through alternative routes. This amounts to about one-third of the new teachers being hired across the United States in that year.[31]

If one had to summarize the research that has been conducted on the effectiveness of alternatively certified teachers, one would describe it as inconclusive. A few studies have examined specific alternative programs, such as Teach For America (TFA) and the New York City Teaching Fellows (NYCTF) program. For example, in one of the more recent studies, researchers from Mathematica Policy Associates compared TFA teachers with control teachers who had never been part of TFA.[32] This means that the control group included traditionally trained teachers, teachers from other alternative programs, and uncertified teachers. The TFA group included both current and former members who had remained teaching beyond the 2 years required for TFA teachers. TFA targets recruits with particularly strong academic records and leadership capabilities, whether or not they have planned to teach or have taken education courses, and hopes especially to attract those who would not otherwise have considered teaching as a career. Thus, most TFA teachers were not education majors in college and will probably go on to pursue careers outside of education. The teacher training provided to TFA recruits is limited in duration, although intensive. They attend a 5-week TFA summer institute to prepare them for their first teaching job at the start of the school year. The institute includes courses on teaching practice, classroom management, diversity, learning theory, literacy development, and leadership. Actual teaching practice takes place in classes of summer school students. Participants also meet regularly with learning teams and attend various evening workshops, with their progress evaluated through regular assessment and feedback provided by institute faculty. For most TFA corps members, training and mentoring continues after they are placed in their classrooms, partly because many states and districts require it. Linda Darling-Hammond noted in 1997 that four separate studies of TFA teachers showed that this minimal training is not enough to prepare them to succeed with students "despite the noticeable intelligence and enthusiasm of many of the recruits."[33]

The Mathematica study found that TFA teachers had stronger academic backgrounds (as measured by the *Barron's* profile) than the control group, had less education-specific training, and tended to earn their education degrees while they were teaching. Also, TFA teachers had less student teaching experience than many, but not all, control teachers. It should be noted that TFA teachers tend to be placed in poor schools, where the general quality of the teachers is usually lower than the national average. Contrary to the research referenced by Darling-Hammond, the Mathematica study found that TFA teachers had a positive impact on math achievement (student scores were significantly higher for TFA teachers than controls) but in reading there were no differences.

One earlier study conducted by a group from the Hoover Institution of Stanford University had also found a slight advantage for TFA teachers working in the Houston Independent School District. Their study has received some criticism (most notably by Linda Darling-Hammond) because they compared TFA teachers not with traditionally certified teachers (although they had the data to do this), but with other uncertified teachers, many of whom did not even have bachelor's degrees.[34] Others have found fault with this study because they did not make available the raw data for other scientists to analyze, and their report was not published in a refereed journal.[35] Another study that did compare TFA teachers with certified teachers found significantly higher scores for the students of certified teachers.[36]

In their study of New York City teachers, Tom Kane and colleagues looked at the effectiveness of alternative preparation by comparing NYCTF teachers with other teachers in the New York City schools.[37] The recruitment and training of Teaching Fellows is similar to that of the TFA teachers. Both programs tend to select students with higher academic performance. NCTF recruits are selected in a three-step process. First, applicants submit background and academic information together with a personal essay. About 60% of the applicants are then invited for an interview. The interview process lasts up to 5 hours, during which time the applicants must teach a 5-minute lesson on a subject of their choice, participate in a guided discussion, write an essay on an unprepared topic, and undergo a one-on-one interview. About half then advance to the final stage, where a committee reviews the applications and offers positions to about 85%. About a quarter do not take up the offers, and a further 15% of those accepting offers do not complete the training for alternative certification. In total, less than 15% of all applicants become Teaching Fellows. Accepted Teaching Fellows attend a 7-week summer training course and assist in a summer school classroom. They must also pass New York State certification examinations and begin coursework in a certification program in an approved graduate school of education.

As we saw from their conclusions about certification status in the previous section, Kane and colleagues had concluded that it was more important to examine within-group differences and the changes in effectiveness of the teachers over time than initial certification status. This finding applies equally to the comparison between traditionally prepared teachers and those in the Fellows program. They found that the NYCTF teachers were no less effective than traditionally prepared teachers, but there was a large range in effectiveness among the Fellows, such that the top quartile of elementary math teachers had value-added scores that were one-third of a standard deviation higher than those of teachers in the bottom quartile.[38]

Another study of NYCTF teachers also produced somewhat mixed findings.[39] Focusing primarily on NYCTF and TFA teachers, these authors found that they sometimes produced higher student achievement gains than the temporary-license teachers they replaced. The findings only applied in certain grades and subjects. More typically, the TFA and NYCTF teachers appeared to be no more or less effective than the temporary-license teachers. When compared with traditionally prepared teachers, the alternatively prepared teachers tended to show lower effectiveness at first, catching up as their experience progressed. Any differences found by the researchers were small. They also noted that the within-group differences were far greater.

The studies of specific alternative preparation programs tend to find that students of these teachers perform the same as or slightly better than those of traditionally prepared teachers, but any differences are quite small. Furthermore, most of the studies have been conducted on programs such as TFA and NYCTF that selectively recruit high-performing graduates from top universities, whereas typical alternative preparation programs are less selective.[40] Thus, the generalizability of these studies is restricted.

A more recent study from Mathematica Policy Research (MPR) attempted to address most of the issues that limited the findings from previous studies of alternative preparation programs.[41] First, MPR did not limit the study to teachers from just one or two alterative programs. Second, they redefined traditionally (TC) and alternatively certified (AC) programs according to whether they required certification before teaching or allowed teaching to begin before certification had been acquired. They then measured the selectivity and amount of coursework provided by the programs. They ruled out the highly selective AC programs from the study, arguing that any differences between those teachers and TC teachers may arise from pre-training characteristics rather than the quality of the training itself. Since the amount of coursework required of AC programs varies by state and district, they included this factor in their analysis. Some AC programs allowed for as many coursework hours as some traditional programs, making it possible to measure whether the level of coursework required as part of teacher certification was related to student achievement, regardless of preparation type. Third, they randomly assigned students to either a TC or AC teacher. They were able to do this because they had a relatively small sample (174 elementary teachers) and they selected schools that hire a large number of AC teachers. The three main findings of the study were: There was no statistically significant difference between the effectiveness of AC and TC teachers, as measured by student achievement gains; greater amounts of coursework appeared to make no difference in the performance of the AC teachers; and the content of the coursework was not associated with teacher effectiveness.

These findings would appear to have fundamental implications for advocates of both kinds of preparation program. However, at least one criticism of the study highlights a number of significant problems with the research that may lead one to think seriously before taking action based on the findings.[42] Sean Corcoran, an educational economist, and Jennifer Jennings, a sociologist, in a lengthy and somewhat scathing review of the Mathematica study, offer three main criticisms: a) The authors ignored or underemphasized in their report analyses that showed advantages in favor of the TC teachers over the AC teachers; b) The sample was problematic because it was small, and the AC and TC teachers had too many overlapping elements in their preparation such that the two groups were not sufficiently distinct; c) And because they drew their sample from an atypical group of schools that hire large numbers of AC teachers, the results are not generalizable to the majority of states, districts, and schools where hiring is more selective. The typically inner-city schools in the study sample had a 91% minority enrollment, had below-average achievement, and, according to Corcoran and Jennings, the TC teachers who served alongside the many AC teachers were probably "substantially less qualified" than the average certified teacher.[43] A further point to note about the Mathematica study is that the teachers had an average of 3 years' experience. Previous studies comparing AC and TC teachers had found the greatest differences in the first 2 years.

Test Scores

Independent of type of program, degree, or institution, the scores that teachers attain on various subject-matter, licensure, or verbal skills tests may constitute a qualification that is indicative of teaching effectiveness. A few researchers have considered test-score variables in their studies. As with the other kinds of qualifications I have examined, results on test scores are mixed. An early study of teachers' verbal skills found no relationship between teachers' word test scores and student achievement gains.[44] Further analysis of the same data by Eric Hanushek found that teachers' word test scores were related to students' reading scores but not vocabulary gains.[45] A few studies looked at teachers' scores on licensure tests. Ronald Ferguson, with colleagues, has been looking for almost 2 decades at the ability of teacher test scores to predict student achievement. In the early 1990s, he found that Texas teachers' performance on the Texas Examination of Current Administrators and Teachers (TECAT), a verbal skills test, predicted student reading and math achievement in some school districts. Later that decade, he found similar results for Alabama using data from the teachers' college entrance exam scores (ACT). In summarizing his own and others' research, he concluded that: "Simply stated, even though the number of studies is relatively small, it appears generally that teachers who score higher on tests produce students who do also."[46]

Eric Hanushek and Steven Rivkin reviewed the estimated effects of teacher test scores on student performance across nine studies that had used value-added methodology. They found the majority of estimates were statistically insignificant; some were significant on the positive side and a smaller number were significant on the negative side. They concluded that the evidence is not overwhelming, represents a range of focus and content, and accounts for only a small proportion of teacher effectiveness.[47]

Most recently, the team led by Clotfelter that studied teachers in North Carolina found that scores on the licensure tests were statistically significantly correlated with student math scores, but at a level that had no practical importance.[48] Harris and Sass, in another analysis of the Florida teacher data, found that teachers' SAT verbal and quantitative scores had no impact on student achievement.[49]

Pedagogical Content Knowledge

Subtly different from having majored in a subject or scoring well on a test of subject matter is being in possession of the knowledge necessary for teaching that subject matter effectively in K–12 classrooms.[50] For some time, pedagogical content knowledge has been the focus of Heather Hill, Brian Rowan, and Deborah Loewenberg Ball at the University of Michigan. They used a survey to assess practicing teachers' mathematical knowledge for teaching math. Having controlled for other teacher and student variables, they found that significantly better student results were associated with higher levels of teachers' math knowledge. The scores on the measure of mathematical knowledge were, in fact, better predictors of effectiveness than other factors such as preparation program and certification, or even the amount of time spent teaching mathematics each day.[51] This finding fits the trend of results that show a relationship between mathematics skills or training or test scores and teacher effectiveness. Similarly, an earlier study led by Brian Rowan that analyzed NELS:88 data found that teachers' subject-matter knowledge had small but significant effects on student achievement in math, especially among low-performing students.[52]

The Betts et al. study of San Diego teachers found that, in middle and high school, the best predictor of effectiveness was teachers' mathematical "board resolution math authorization"—in other words, a formal indication of their subject-matter knowledge in math.[53] Harris and Sass found in their study of Florida teachers that pedagogical content knowledge was positively associated with student achievement test scores in math, but at the elementary and middle school grades, not high school.[54] Also, the study by David Monk in which he analyzed NAEP data showed that mathematics pedagogy courses made teachers more effective in raising student achievement. The relationship did not show up for science.[55]

Level of Professional Development

Professional development in the form of courses, seminars, or workshops represents another arrow in the quiver of qualifications that teachers may possess, albeit obtained after they have started practicing. This was one of the variables of interest in a study on instructional policy conducted by researchers at the University of Michigan, David Cohen and Heather Hill. They analyzed data on elementary teachers in California using a 1994 survey they had administered while on a project at Michigan State University, together with the state of California's Learning Assessment System (CLAS) test scores. They found a "modest" relationship between workshop attendance in general and student achievement, but no apparent effect for participation in subject-specific workshops, a result they believed was of greater importance.[56]

Harold Wenglinsky, conversely, in his analysis of NAEP data, found significant relationships between student achievement in math and science and specific types of professional development. For math, professional development in working with students from special populations, and higher-order thinking skills, were most important. In science, the important topic was laboratory skills.[57]

Patricia Kannapel and Stephen Clements were funded by the Ford Foundation to "audit" eight high-poverty elementary schools in Kentucky that had records of high performance in order to determine what factors may account for their ability to break the pattern of low achievement usually associated with such schools. An audit involves school visits by a team of experts including researcher, administrator, professor, teacher, and parent. Kannapel and Clements collected data through interviews, classroom observation, and the review of materials. Their results were compared with state audits of similar schools. They found that ongoing, job-embedded professional development that was connected to student achievement data distinguished the high-performing from the low-performing schools.[58]

One study found no effect for professional development. In this case, the authors were studying teachers in high-poverty, rural schools in northeastern Brazil. They found that teachers' participation in professional development had no effect on student achievement, although this may have been because mostly underqualified teachers were selected to take part in the training workshops.[59]

Teaching Experience

Studies of the importance of teaching experience in determining student achievement are perhaps the most numerous among the research on teacher qualifications and teacher effectiveness. Strictly speaking, experience and professional development do not necessarily belong among a group of variables described as "front-end qualifications" unless one is thinking from the perspective of a school administrator who is considering an applicant pool of teachers that may vary according to their existing teaching experience. For the purposes of this review, I therefore include both these variables here. Teaching experience is usually defined by the number of years a teacher has spent in the classroom.

Richard Murnane (sometimes with Barbara Philips) conducted a number of early studies examining the relationship between teaching experience and teaching effectiveness. Murnane first studied elementary teachers in an inner-city setting and found that teacher effectiveness increased sharply over the first 3 years and peaked at 5 years.[60] In a later study, Murnane and Philips postulated two variables that might influence the effects of "learning by doing" or gaining expertise through the act of teaching. These two variables were "vintage" and "selection effects." Vintage effect (sometimes called cohort effect) refers to the fact that teachers may be hired in years of shortage or glut, and this will influence the quality of the teacher pool available to districts in need of teachers, and thus confound the effects of experience. Selection effects refer to the possibility that more effective teachers may leave to become administrators or take better-paying jobs in other professions, so mitigating any positive effects of learning by doing. Murnane and Philips were only able to control for vintage effects, but when they added this variable to the model, they found that the relationship between experience and performance changed from non-significant to significant. In a second study published the same year (1981), the authors found, when controlling for other variables, that experience was related to student achievement as follows: positive during the first 7 years, negative from years 8 to 14, and positive for 15 years plus. These findings are explained again by learning by doing and vintage effects.

Other researchers have also found some degree of positive relationship between experience and student achievement in math and reading, especially in the early years. Brian Rowan and colleagues from the University of Michigan analyzed data from the Prospects National Longitudinal Study.[61] They found very small positive effects for teaching experience and reading growth among teachers of grades 1–6, and mathematics growth among grades 3–6.[62] Linda Cavalluzzo, in her aforementioned study of NBC teachers in Miami-Dade, Florida, found that experience (along with all other teacher-quality indicators except for undergraduate school selectivity) was significantly positively correlated with student achievement.[63]

In a more recent study from 2004, Jonah Rockoff had access to teacher and student data over a period of 12 years, with 5 years of annual test scores from elementary students in a number of schools. These data enabled him to credibly identify teacher-fixed effects (to paraphrase his words), thus making up for weaknesses in previous studies that did not allow the separation of classroom effects from teacher effects, since data limitations restricted researchers to examining teachers with only one classroom's worth of data.[64] Eric Hanushek had also made this point, as one of the first to use fixed effects when analyzing student achievement.[65] Rockoff found that 10 years of teaching experience is expected to raise both Vocabulary and Reading Comprehension test scores by about 4 NCE points, or 0.2 standard deviations. For Mathematics Computation, experience raises scores in the first 2 years, but subsequent years appear to lower scores. For Mathematics Concepts, no relation to experience was observed. Rockoff discussed the implications of these findings in the context of teacher quality, concluding that hiring and compensating teachers purely on the basis of education and experience beyond the first few years is unlikely to result in desired increases in school effectiveness.

A few researchers have found no differences between more and less experienced teachers. Matthew Carr, in a policy report for the Buckeye Institute,[66] presented results on data from Ohio teachers, disaggregated by whether they taught in traditional or charter schools. His findings on charter schools found no meaningful relationships between any of the teacher qualifications and student achievement. In a study of a single charter school in Los Angeles, Alix Gallagher also found no effect of teaching experience on student achievement.[67] For teachers in traditional public schools, the NCLB definition of "highly qualified" was the most important factor, whereas years of experience (or a master's degree) was not. This led Carr to conclude:

> We need teachers who know their subjects and who have proven their competency over the subjects they teach more than we need teachers with higher levels of experience or higher levels of degree attainment.[68]

Carr further emphasized the importance of distinguishing between traditional and charter schools when considering educational data. From Carr's descriptive statistics, one can see that the traditional and charter schools differed significantly on a number of variables that may have influenced the findings. Teachers in traditional schools were considerably more experienced, were more likely to have higher degrees, were more likely to be rated high-quality, and taught lower percentages of Black and disadvantaged students.

Over the years, Eric Hanushek and various colleagues have conducted and reviewed many studies that included the variable of teacher experience and its connection with student achievement.[69] A summary of Hanushek's work and the studies reviewed in a 2006 book chapter written with Steven Rivkin leads to the following conclusions:

1. While the general trend is toward a positive relationship between experience and student achievement, it is not a strong one;
2. In most studies that find a positive effect it does not reach statistical significance;
3. Many studies may be faulted because they look at contemporaneous measures of teachers and schools rather than value-added measures over several years;
4. Studies do not take into account differences in teacher quality related to differences in state credentialing requirements;
5. Even the value-added studies that show positive relationships have small effect sizes.[70]

Teacher Qualifications—Summary

When performance data are not available, it is through teacher qualifications that states and districts control who is permitted and selected to teach in their classrooms. From the many studies that have attempted to measure the relationship between various kinds of qualification and student achievement, we may conclude only that certain types of qualification appear to make a difference and only under certain circumstances. In particular, qualifications that are associated with greater mathematics knowledge (certification, test scores, advanced degrees, pedagogical content knowledge) appear to produce teachers whose students have better math achievement than students of teachers without those qualifications. Among the other variables reviewed, experience appears to have an effect during the early years of teaching across the majority of studies, while the remaining evidence is mixed at best.

The mixed evidence on the effects of certification on teacher effectiveness has produced quite controversial rhetoric. The variety of findings may partly be a reflection of the different criteria required for certification across states. Thus, being a certified teacher implies a wide range of possible qualifications. Furthermore, certification in some settings may be awarded to alternatively prepared teachers based on requirements that differ from those who are traditionally prepared. The studies reporting a positive relationship between certification and teacher effectiveness are those that look at subject-specific certification in mathematics, particularly among the upper grade levels. Studies comparing certified and uncertified teachers often find no advantage for certification. These studies rely upon the situations that exist in school systems where lack of certification probably reflects the difficulty of hiring high-quality teachers to work in hard-to-staff schools that have large populations of students from low-income and limited-English-speaking families. On the other hand, with one exception, the studies comparing traditional and alternative preparation and certification have focused on programs such as TFA and NYCTF that actively recruit high-performing students from top institutions. In both situations, the selection factors complicate the interpretation of any findings and reduce or nullify their generalizability.

The vigorous debate about the role of certification in producing effective teachers dates back to a 1996 report from the National Commission on Teaching and America's Future (NCTAF).[71] The NCTAF report drew attention to the need for qualified teachers in the United States by arguing that the country should aim to be more like countries in Europe and Asia where teachers are more highly respected, better prepared, and better compensated. It noted the large numbers of teachers in American schools who had no or emergency certification nor a college major or minor in their field (especially in math), were teaching out of field (particularly in science, math, and English), and were likely to be unlicensed if they taught in high-minority schools.[72] The argument for the importance of certification was contested in a couple of spirited documents written by the Abell Foundation's[73] Kate Walsh, a policy analyst who has since become the president of the National Council on Teacher Quality (NCTQ).[74] Walsh's report was followed by a response from Darling-Hammond and a rejoinder from Kate Walsh aided by Michael Podgursky.[75]

Walsh found fault with the research upon which Darling-Hammond based her recommendations in the NCTAF report, quoting other studies that gave counterevidence. Darling-Hammond defended her report, accusing Walsh, among other things, of misreading her findings, omitting a large number of studies from her review, and ignoring evidence from the studies she did cite. Walsh came back with a defense for each of the criticisms. I recommend that anyone interested in the topic download the articles and review the exchanges. I leave it to the reader to decide which side has the greater credibility. Suffice it to say that no one is usually wholly right or wrong in this kind of polemic. Incidentally, Darling-Hammond, along with Barnett Berry representing NCTAF and Amy Thoreson of the University of Chicago, responded in a less acrimonious fashion to the findings of Dan Goldhaber and Dominic Brewer, who, as we saw earlier, had determined from their analyses of the NELS:88 data that teachers with emergency certification were no less effective than traditionally certified teachers. Darling-Hammond and colleagues disputed this finding, maintaining that there were methodological problems in their analysis and that the small sample of NELS:88 teachers in the emergency-credentialed category had qualifications that resembled those of traditionally certified teachers.[76] Darling-Hammond's later study in the Houston schools concluded that certified teachers consistently produced stronger student achievement gains than uncertified teachers.[77]

The findings on advanced certification are equally confusing, although they haven't provoked any heated dialogue. Attainment of National Board Certification seems to correlate with math achievement in high school, and both math and reading achievement in middle school. If you compare NBC teachers with those who have never attempted the application, you will find no differences in effectiveness, since variations within groups are likely to be greater than the variations between them. Attaining NBC status does not result in an increase in effectiveness.

In general, although a number of studies suggest that certification is linked to teacher effectiveness, there are as many or more studies that find certification does not predict a teacher's ability to raise student achievement. This lack of consensus suggests that, whoever wins the argument about which studies are more compelling, we have yet to discover exactly what attributes certification may be signaling about a teacher's ability to help students learn academic content. The definition of teacher quality in NCLB (full certification, having a bachelor's degree, demonstrating competence in subject matter and teaching) has resulted in considerable variety across states in how they determine whether NCLB requirements are met. This is further exacerbated by what some have described as a loophole in the Department of Education's regulation, which also labels as "highly qualified" teachers who are still "participating in an alternative route to certification." This means that on his or her first day in an alternative-route teacher-credentialing program, a teacher-in-training could be considered "highly qualified." The possibility that students may, under this definition, be taught by unprepared teachers prompted a coalition of plaintiffs, including Californians for Justice, California ACORN, and several students and parents, to file suit in August 2007 in the federal district court of San Francisco in the case known as *Renee v. Spellings*. The case was subsequently ruled in favor of the defendant in summary judgment by Judge Phyllis Hamilton in June 2008.[78]

Although it seems NCLB was on the right track in requiring teachers to be proficient in the subject matter and the ability to teach it, any focus on full certification (however defined), requiring specific kinds of undergraduate (or even master's) degrees, and testing teachers on general or specific knowledge, appears to be based on little evidence in support of any relationship to teacher effectiveness as measured by gains in student achievement. Advocates of alternative paths to teacher preparation argue that such requirements end up effectively reducing the supply of teachers by discouraging high-performing students who might not wish to take the courses required for certification.

As of 2010, the Obama administration is in the process of revising NCLB and is putting resources into the measurement of teacher effectiveness rather than the specification of teacher qualifications, an approach that demands a better method for evaluating teachers. We will get to this later in the book. First, we will examine the research on other aspects of teacher quality.

PERSONAL ATTRIBUTES

The personal attributes of teachers include features such as race and gender, personality and attitudes, verbal and second-language skills. Some of these characteristics are fixed, while others are subject to change. The number of research studies linking personal attributes to student achievement is small. As with the research on teacher qualifications, the findings are mixed.

Race

The underrepresentation of minorities among teachers has given rise to recommendations from a variety of sources to devote efforts to the recruitment and retention of racial and ethnic minorities among the K–12 teaching force.[79] The potential benefits of a racial match between teacher and student are usually expressed in terms of either "passive" effects (for example, where a teacher serves as a positive role model) or "active" effects (whereby same-race teachers may have more positive perceptions of and expectations for their students than different race teachers).[80] Although the evidence for or against the existence of these kinds of effects is limited, one study by Thomas Dee using NELS:88 data showed a significant effect of having a demographically similar teacher on the perceptions of a student's performance or behavior. Students who were viewed negatively by teachers performed significantly lower on subject tests, and they were less likely to take Advanced Placement tests. Dee found that the effects associated with race and ethnicity were concentrated among poor students from the South. Although hiring more underrepresented teachers may help ameliorate the problem, it may also have the unintended consequence of harming students who do not share the teacher's race or ethnicity. Thus, Dee recommends appropriate professional development for all teachers that enable them to understand and overcome their potential negative perceptions and expectations.[81]

Addressing another aspect of teacher/student racial match on student achievement, Dee found in a subsequent study (where he was able to look at classes where students had been randomly assigned to teachers) that having a teacher of the same race improves the math and reading achievement of both Black and White students.[82] Eric Hanushek and colleagues also found that Black students perform better when they have Black teachers.[83] These studies would support the hypothesis that Black teachers are likely to have higher expectations of Black students than are White teachers, leading to what is known as the Pygmalion effect, whereby people (in particular children or students) perform better if greater expectations are placed upon them.[84]

Findings such as these lead us to the topic of racial stereotyping and perceptual bias. For an excellent treatment of this subject and the relevant research on its relationship to the Black-White achievement gap, I refer the reader to an article by Ronald Ferguson.[85] A useful contribution of this article is Ferguson's distinction among three criteria for judging bias. First, he distinguishes "unconditionally" from "conditionally" race neutral. Unconditionally race neutral teachers are those who expect the same from Blacks and Whites. Conditionally race neutral teachers may base their neutrality on observable, measurable criteria, such as similar past grades or test scores. Alternatively, neutrality may be based not on past performance but on unobserved potential. Most experiments on bias examine unconditional race neutrality, and the typical finding is that teachers are biased.[86]

Gender

Studies of teacher-student gender match ask questions similar to those that look at race. Role model issues come into play, as do teacher perceptions and expectations. Ronald Ehrenberg and colleagues examined the NELS:88 data in the mid-1990s and had found that neither racial nor gender match was associated with how much the students learned, although, like Dee, they found that these attributes did affect teachers' subjective evaluations of their students.[87] Lucia Nixon and Michael Robinson tested whether role model effects existed for high school girls with female school faculty, using a different database, The National Longitudinal Survey of Youth (NLSY).[88] They found a small positive effect of having female teachers for female students on four different outcomes: highest grade completed, high school graduation, college entry, and college graduation. They concluded that, since these effects were not evident among male students, the findings support their hypothesis that female teachers and professional staff provide positive role models for female students that lead to better academic outcomes.[89]

Personality, Beliefs, and Attitudes

For many years, there have been few investigations of the effects of teacher personality on student outcomes. Jacob Getzels and Philip Jackson concluded that the weaknesses of contemporary psychological tests resulted in the unproductive and chaotic research findings that had appeared up to their 1963 review.[90] Recently, there has been some interest in applying the Myers-Briggs Type Indicator (MBTI)[91] to the field of teaching in order to determine which personality types are associated with teacher effectiveness. In one study, Stephen Rushton and colleagues determined that 58 elementary teachers nominated for their effectiveness to the Florida League of Teachers by their supervising administrators were significantly different in their MBTI profiles from randomly selected elementary teachers in two comparison groups. Specifically, the teachers in the expert group were more likely to exhibit an ENFP profile (extrovert, intuitive, feeling, and perceiving).[92] Although this may be of interest to psychologists, it is not clear how those involved in education could put the information to good use.

Another personal characteristic of teachers related to their beliefs is teacher efficacy. This concept is derived from Julian Rotter's theory of internal versus external control of reinforcement (often known as locus of control)[93] and Albert Bandura's social cognitive theory of self-efficacy.[94] Researchers have identified three different kinds of efficacy. The first is a teacher's belief that the practice of teaching can influence student learning. The second is self-efficacy, the personal belief of a teacher that he or she has the ability to affect student outcomes. The third concept is collective teacher efficacy, defined as "the perceptions of teachers in a school that the efforts of the faculty as a whole will have a positive effect on students."[95]

A few researchers have attempted to look at the effects of teacher efficacy on student achievement. Early research on efficacy reported positive correlations between degree of teacher efficacy and the amount of gain students made on standardized tests of reading.[96] Later studies followed, reporting significant relationships between teachers' degrees of efficacy and student gains on standardized math tests.[97] More recently in 2005, a study that examined National Board certified teachers included a measure of teachers' sense of their own efficacy, but efficacy did not discriminate the more from the less effective teachers, as measured by student achievement gains.[98]

Collective teacher efficacy was examined in another study of teachers from 47 Midwestern schools and was found to be significantly associated with student achievement. However, the authors of the study were not able to rule out the possibility that some other school-related factors might have caused both the elevated collective efficacy and the student achievement levels.[99] Other researchers have looked at the effects of efficacy on teaching practice and found there to be some correlations between efficacy and certain instructional factors.[100] A reasonable concern with any study linking efficacy and student achievement is determining the direction of a relationship. Are strong feelings of efficacy developed in the context of high-achieving students, or do those feelings result in increased achievement? Both explanations are equally likely.

The effects of teacher expectations on student performance became a controversial topic of inquiry in the late 1960s with the publication of *Pygmalion in the Classroom* by Robert Rosenthal and Lenore Jacobson.[101] The book describes an elegant experimental manipulation of teacher expectations for student achievement to see if these expectations would be fulfilled. The results appeared to show that artificially high expectations actually led to enhanced student outcomes, as measured by an IQ test. Subsequent replication attempts failed to reproduce the results, however, and a host of critics found fault with the study design and procedures,[102] the adequacy of the ability test,[103] the sampling procedures, subject attrition, and other details of the analysis.[104] Furthermore, as Lee Jussim and Kent Harber point out, the simple description of Rosenthal and Jacobson's findings that attracted the enthusiastic attention of both academic and lay audiences proved to be misleading when the details of the findings were explored.[105] First, students from both groups (described as late bloomers and controls) increased in IQ levels, so there was no evidence that low expectations actually harmed students. Second, the differences between the two groups were recorded largely among the 1st- and 2nd-graders, while the average across all six grades was only a few percentage points. In spite of these issues, the study was frequently cited as evidence that teachers' expectations of students may lead to self-fulfilling prophecies that discriminate against some and favor others, resulting in potential contributions to widespread social inequalities.[106]

Whether one embraces or rejects the *Pygmalion* study, the notion of the self-fulfilling prophecy and teacher expectations has been tested since by many researchers. A full description of these studies, although interesting, is not justified here, as reviews have been produced over the years by many authors.[107] A brief overview of the main points will suffice.

The idea of the self-fulfilling prophecy originated in the work of the eminent sociologist Robert K. Merton,[108] who defined the concept (which stems from the Thomas Theorem[109]) as "a *false* definition of the situation evoking a new behavior which makes the original false conception come 'true.'"[110] The concept has gained considerable traction in the field of social cognition, and reviews from social psychology typically accept the original conclusions of Rosenthal and Jacobson. Educational psychologists were inclined to be more critical of the findings, often explaining them by claiming that teachers tended to be accurate in their estimations of students, thus attributing to them a degree of insight that undermines the power self-fulfilling prophecies. As we so often find, the truth probably lies somewhere in the middle. From the many studies, we may cautiously conclude that teachers do make self-fulfilling prophecies, but their effects, either on student IQ or achievement, are typically small. These effects do not appear to have any cumulative influence across teachers or over time,[111] are more likely to occur among students from disadvantaged or stigmatized social groups,[112] and may or may not do more harm than good.[113] Ultimately, correlations between teacher expectations and student outcomes may just as often be the result of teachers' accurate assessments as of self-fulfilling prophecies.

Verbal Ability

A discussion of the relative importance of a teacher's verbal ability (facility with the spoken and written word) takes us right to the heart of the recent debate on certification and pedagogical training that we reviewed in the section above on teacher qualifications. The reader will recall that the critics of traditional preparation programs are inclined to suggest that teacher characteristics are more important than pedagogical training. Verbal ability is one of the characteristics most often cited. Content knowledge is another. In his annual report on teacher quality, former education secretary Rod Paige maintained in his quest for highly qualified teachers:

> As Congress made clear through its definition of "highly qualified teachers," and as the scientific evidence supports, the only measurable teacher attributes that relate directly to improved student achievement are high verbal ability and solid content knowledge.... To meet the "highly qualified teachers" challenge, then, states will need to streamline their certification system to focus on the few things that really matter: verbal ability, content knowledge, and, as a safety precaution, a background check of new teachers.[114]

Since teachers must be able to explain concepts and present information clearly to help their students improve their oral and written skills and to communicate effectively with parents and administrators, a level of verbal ability is a necessary requirement for being an effective teacher. But that is not to say it is a sufficient requirement.

The "scientific evidence" referred to in the government report was mostly collected 25–50 years ago, in particular by the authors of the well-known Coleman report[115] and by Ronald Ferguson, who studied data from 900 school districts in Texas.[116] Linda Darling-Hammond and Peter Youngs present a rebuttal to Paige's 2002 report (and to the arguments of Kate Walsh) in the "Research News and Comment" section of the *Educational Researcher* later that same year.[117] The Coleman report limited its findings to Black students, was only apparent at two grade levels (3 and 6), and used a vocabulary test as a measure of verbal ability.[118] The Coleman data were reanalyzed by many researchers, including Ronald Ehrenberg and Dominic Brewer.[119] These researchers created synthetic gain scores and found that an increase in teachers' verbal aptitude was related to student gains in the elementary grades. They noted the limitations of the ancient database and the reliance on synthetic gain scores.

Ferguson's measure of verbal ability was the Texas Examination of Current Administrators (TECAT), primarily a test of literacy skills based on responses to a written passage. He reported that average TECAT scores explained up to 25% of a district's average reading scores in all but 1st grade (which means that three-quarters of the variance must have been explained by factors other than verbal ability).

The Ehrenberg and Brewer study referenced in the section above on the influence of college status on teacher effectiveness postulated that "institutional selectivity is a proxy for the verbal ability, or intelligence, of the teachers in the school."[120] They went on to assert that they therefore provided "indirect evidence of the importance of verbal ability in the educational process."

Another more recent study on verbal ability and teacher effectiveness was conducted in 2005 by Michael Andrew and colleagues at the University of New Hampshire.[121] They studied 116 teacher interns across a variety of disciplines, measuring verbal ability with the Graduate Record Examination—Verbal scores. Teacher effectiveness was measured not by student test scores but by supervisor ratings of teachers' performance in the classroom. They found that verbal ability was only correlated with the lowest-performing interns, suggesting that verbal skills are necessary but not sufficient for effective teaching. It remains to be seen whether this finding bears out when student outcomes constitute the dependent variable.

The mixed findings on verbal ability and teacher effectiveness reflect those on test scores in general. In their review of the literature on this topic, Andrew Wayne and Peter Youngs explained the divergent findings in the studies they reviewed by examining the controls used by the researchers.[122] When college ratings were controlled, negative findings were obtained. The studies that found positive results for test scores and verbal ability did not control for this factor, suggesting that college ratings capture a dimension of teacher quality similar to that represented by test scores. It looks as if tested verbal ability is likely to affect teacher quality if college ratings have not already been accounted for.

Personal Attributes: Summary

The relatively few studies in this section have mixed findings and achieve little consensus. The wide range of personal attributes that have been the subject of study, together with the fact that many of them are impervious to change, suggest that this may be the least promising area for research, while at the same time leaving us with the greatest number of unanswered questions.

PEDAGOGICAL PRACTICE

The studies in this group examine the extent to which the *process* of teaching—that is, the strategies and practices that teachers use—relates to student achievement. Research on this aspect of teacher quality is challenging because methods of evaluating teacher practice typically involve either classroom observation, a task that brings with it a whole raft of complications; surveys and questionnaires, which suffer from the biases associated with self-report data; or a collection of classroom artifacts, which is likely to be a cumbersome process that is difficult to standardize. We will be looking in more detail at these factors as they relate to teacher evaluation in Chapter 4. Although most studies that focus on teaching practice find some sort of positive connection between teachers' strategies and student achievement, the significance of their findings tends to be either low or compromised by design or instrumentation problems.

Studies Based on Classroom Observation

In the largest group of studies from this category, researchers used modified versions of Charlotte Danielson's Framework for Teaching as a means for measuring the effects of teaching practice through classroom observation.[123] The Danielson Framework consists of four domains of teaching that go beyond elements of practice that are observable through classroom observation. They are: planning and preparation, the classroom environment, instruction, and professional responsibilities. In addition to observing teachers teach, users of this protocol also collect logs and portfolios of work. Herbert Heneman and colleagues (associated with the Consortium for Policy Research in Education, or CPRE) assessed the correlation between teacher scores on the Framework and value-added student achievement scores as part of a study examining the possibility of providing skill-based pay to teachers.[124] The instrument was used, in varying modifications, across several school sites in different states (Los Angeles; Cincinnati; Reno, Nevada; and Coventry, Rhode Island), each of which had been studied by other researchers individually. The research studies showed positive correlations between evaluation scores and student achievement averaged over 3 years, ranging from a high of 0.37 for reading in the Los Angeles school to a low of 0.11 in math for the Coventry site. The authors suggested that the disparate findings across sites might be due partially to the quality and number of evaluators. In Cincinnati, the evaluators were highly trained, and in the Los Angeles charter school the teachers had a unified view of quality teaching, while in the other sites a single evaluator conducted the observations and had less training.

Geoffrey Borman and colleagues in an earlier CPRE study examined data from the Washoe County School District in Nevada, where they also used a version of the Danielson Framework to which they had made only "minor changes."[125] They looked at 130-plus teachers in each of the 4th, 5th, and 6th grades and found that teachers at the highest end on the Danielson instrument had students who achieved at slightly higher levels than teachers at the lowest end. Correlations between observational evaluation and student achievement at levels as low as this are of little use in measuring teacher effectiveness. A related study of Washoe County data also found low, mostly statistically insignificant, correlations between teacher practices as measured by four of Danielson's Framework scales and 3rd- to 5th-grade student achievement.[126] Either the measure is not distinguishing the most critical teaching practices, the tests are not measuring what the teacher is teaching, or other factors are influencing student test performance. Elizabeth Holztapple obtained similar results in her analysis of the data from Cincinnati Public Schools.[127] H. Alix Gallagher found relationships between literacy and composite evaluation scores with student achievement in the Los Angeles charter school, but no correlations with mathematics and language arts scores. After interviewing some of the teachers, he concluded that there may have been more consistency and alignment in their pedagogical approaches to literacy.[128] Anthony Milanowski's study of Cincinnati data found correlations ranging from 0.27 to 0.43 between evaluations on the Framework-based instrument and student growth.[129]

Not all researchers who measured teaching practice through observation used the Danielson instrument. Lindsay Matsumura and colleagues administered the Instructional Quality Assessment (IQA) toolkit with 34 teachers in urban middle schools.[130] The IQA toolkit includes analyses of teacher assignments and student work samples in addition to observations. The quality of instruction varied across schools and the IQA predicted some reading and vocabulary scores (on the Stanford Achievement Test, 10th Edition), and the observation component predicted mathematics achievement. The sample size was too small and the trends of the findings were too restricted to enable use of the instrument to make practical predictions about teaching effectiveness as related to student achievement.

John Schachter and Yeow Meng Thum reviewed the teaching strategies research and developed their own set of five teaching standards and performance rubrics: grouping students, thinking, activities, motivating students, and teacher knowledge of students. From these, they identified 12 performance standards and rubrics to measure teacher quality. Trained graduate students observed 52 volunteer teachers across grades 3–6 using the rubric during several scheduled and unscheduled classroom visits over the school year. They examined the relationship between the ratings and student gains in reading, mathematics, and language arts. In spite of a wide range of teaching quality in their sample, the authors calculated that one standard deviation increase in teaching quality translated to increased class achievement gains of 6.80 points in language, 7.06 points in mathematics, and 4.73 points in reading.[131] This relationship is substantially higher than those found by other researchers.

Brian Jacob and Lars Lefgren sought to determine whether school principals could identify effective teachers, as defined by value-added scores.[132] They found that principals were better able to predict the effectiveness of 202 teachers than were paper qualifications such as education and experience. However, the principals used all information at their disposal, not just classroom observations. Also, they were more accurate with the highest- and lowest-rated teachers and not accurate with the teachers in the middle range of effectiveness. Furthermore, male teachers and untenured teachers tended to be rated less effective than the rankings from their achievement gains, suggesting that the principals were open to biases.

Patricia Kannapel and Stephen Clements used the Kentucky State audit system[133] to compare more and less successful high-poverty schools in the state, based on state data.[134] They determined that the teachers in the more successful schools exhibited certain teaching practices: They were more likely to conduct frequent assessments and offer feedback; tended to deliver instruction aligned with learning goals, assessments, and diverse learning styles; demonstrated higher expectations for student performance; participated more in collaborative decision making and ongoing, job-embedded professional development; and more often used student achievement data for staff development purposes. As with the Jacob and Lefgren study, the audit team had more information to work with than could be obtained through classroom observations alone. Also, the dependent variable was overall school performance, and findings were averaged across teachers.

Studies Based on Teacher Surveys

Instead of observing classrooms, some researchers choose to interview teachers in order to find out information about their practice. Although this is less time consuming than observing classrooms, it is also potentially less reliable. In two such studies, researchers analyzed whether math test scores were higher when the teacher reported using instructional practices related to reform standards, in one case those developed by the state of California[135] and in the second by the National Council of Teachers of Mathematics (NCTM).[136]

The first study was conducted by David Cohen and Heather Hill.[137] They measured teachers' use of instructional practices in math from data collected in a 14-item survey of a stratified sample of 975 California elementary teachers in 1994 (of whom 595 responded). They focused on whether teachers were using conventional or reform practices and looked to see if self-reported practice was related to improved student achievement on California's math test (California Learning Assessment System, or CLAS). They found a moderate relationship, and also that attendance at workshops, use of replacement units, and learning about CLAS were also related to higher math scores. Conclusions from this study are necessarily limited by the reliance on self-report data, the use of absolute rather than value-added or gain scores, a mediocre response rate to the survey, and the aggregation of data.

A second study used self-report teacher survey data to correlate reform instructional practices in math with student achievement among 10th-graders. Dan McCaffrey and colleagues surveyed 225 teachers in a large urban school district (of whom 220 responded). Regression analyses determined that test scores were higher for students in integrated mathematics courses when teachers used the reform practices more often, but not in other more traditional algebra and geometry courses that were not designed to be consistent with the NCTM reforms. Although the same reservations about self-report data apply to this study, the response rate was high, and other variables were controlled. The authors concluded that reforms in teaching practice should be accompanied by appropriate changes in curriculum.

Harold Wenglinsky took advantage of the NAEP[138] survey dataset to examine the relationship between teacher quality and student performance in the 8th grade. Using multi-level modeling, he looked at classroom practices, professional development, and teacher characteristics such as education level and experience. Overall, Wenglinsky found that classroom practices were more closely related to student performance than the other variables. His study was somewhat limited by the fact that test scores and teacher variables were measured cross-sectionally rather than longitudinally. Thus, we cannot know whether enhanced practices led to greater student achievement or that having higher-achieving students allowed the teachers to conduct more advanced strategies. Also, he studied only one grade level and relied on aggregated school data to determine teacher practice.

Some studies look at a particular teaching practice or approach. One study in England, for example, looked at the effect of a new practice for teaching elementary reading called the "literacy hour."[139] The National Literacy Project introduced the literacy hour to around 400 English primary schools in 1997 and 1998. It involved both an innovation in curriculum as well as practice.[140] Key elements of practice derived from multiple research studies included "structured teaching" (making clear what has to be learned, dividing material into manageable units, teaching in a well-considered sequence, encouraging students to use hunches and prompts, and regular testing for progress) and "effective learning time" (whole-class teaching can often be superior to individualized teaching).[141] The authors of this study compared the progress of students in literacy hour schools with control students not in the program, and, controlling for potential intervening factors, found that the literacy hour significantly increased reading skills by about 2–3 percentage points. However, the highest-ability students were unaffected by the literacy hour program, suggesting that the greater rigidity of the structure holds those students back.

An even more focused study was conducted by German economists Guido Schwerdt and Amelie Wuppermann from the University of Munich.[142] They tested whether traditional lecture-style teaching in U.S. middle schools is less effective than the alternative practices based on active and problem-oriented learning embodied in the teaching standards that focus on hands-on learning and group work, advocated by the National Council of Teachers of Mathematics (NCTM).[143] The authors analyzed 2003 Trends in International Mathematics and Science Study (TIMSS)[144] data to determine differences among teachers with regard to teaching time devoted to lecture-style presentation or in-class problem-solving. They found that a 10-percentage point shift from problem-solving to lecture-style presentation resulted in an increase in science and mathematics student achievement of about 1% of a standard deviation. They concluded that traditional lecture-style teaching is not detrimental to student learning, and that achievement levels are therefore unlikely to be raised by increased use of the alternative practices advocated by NCTM.

Another teaching strategy study was conducted among 339 grade 8 teachers from a stratified sample of 65 schools in Pakistan by two research economists from Oxford University.[145] The researchers asked teachers a number of questions about teaching practice, including amount of time giving quizzes, reviewing homework, writing on the blackboard, and whether they used lesson plans, asked frequent questions, and read aloud from notes or books while teaching. They found that, perhaps not surprisingly, teachers who reportedly spent more time on lesson planning and those who asked more questions in class had students with higher test scores.

Studies Based on Student Surveys

Another source of information on teacher practice may be obtained by polling students, and a few researchers have elected to use this option. Part of the rationale for using students as a source of information is that teachers often overestimate their use of effective practices. This view is borne out in data collected by Pamela Frome and colleagues of the Research Triangle Institute, using data from the Southern Regional Board of Education (SREB), and reported in a research brief from SREB.[146] The researchers studied a number of teacher-quality indicators among 1,210 middle-grade teachers of mathematics, science, and language arts, including teaching practice. Use of certain "effective" teaching strategies (such as "solve mathematics problems other than from textbooks," or "explain different ways for solving mathematics problems") when reported by students were found to be related to student achievement. When use of similar teaching practices was reported by teachers, there was no relationship. This could be explained by the fact that the teacher data could not be linked to students and had to be aggregated at the school level, a limitation of the study. Teachers may also overestimate their use of effective strategies.

A second study measuring student perceptions of teacher practice used data from more than 1,000 8th-grade students in Cyprus collected as part of the third TIMSS Study, conducted in 2003. Among other things, the student survey measured "classroom processes" by collecting perceptions of the "strategies and practices teachers use in helping students learn."[147] These included items related to the extent to which students work on projects in class, discuss practical problems, and work on problems related to daily life. Other items asked about homework assignments and the alignment of assessment and curricular practices. The resulting correlation between these practices and student achievement was negligible, and one could not infer any causality because there were no controls for prior performance of students or schools.

Pedagogical Practice—Summary

Learning what teachers actually do when they conduct their lessons is perhaps the most important key to understanding the effects that teachers have on student learning. All other variables affect how teachers behave. Education, training, personal characteristics, experience, curriculum, and the interaction of these variables with the characteristics of the students, the school, and the community all serve to influence how a teacher performs in the classroom, the strategies used, the choices made, and the level of motivation and enthusiasm that goes into the teaching. The challenge is how best to collect information about teacher practice, and how to relate what we find to student learning. As we can see from the glimpse of existing research, these are still open questions.

TEACHER EFFECTIVENESS

As noted, teacher effectiveness is the outcome variable for the studies in the previous sections and so some of the studies described here might also belong in one of the earlier sections. In an apparently circular argument, some studies seek to show that a teacher's value-added effectiveness[148] is predictive of subsequent achievement of students in that teacher's class, thereby leading to the claim that high-quality teachers are those who show the greatest effectiveness. Other studies described in this section seek to demonstrate the existence of differences in teacher effectiveness as measured by student achievement gains and show how they might correlate with observable variables such as teacher qualifications, characteristics, or experience, or so-called unobservables (i.e., unobservable aspects of teacher quality).

Effectiveness as Measured by Student Achievement

The current national focus on measuring teacher effectiveness as expressed by an ability to raise student achievement with the possible intention of using the information for high-stakes personnel decisions makes these studies of particular relevance to policymakers.

One of the most recent studies of this kind at the time of writing was conducted by Dan Goldhaber and Michael Hansen.[149] They obtained access to an 11-year panel of data from North Carolina schools where student test scores were linked to teachers. Their sample consisted of 556 4th- to 5th-grade teachers with 3,442 unique teacher-year observations. One of their three research questions was focused on the extent to which early-career job performance serves as a signal of performance later in teacher careers. The goal of their study was to investigate the potential of using VAM[150] estimates to make tenure decisions for teachers.

Their use of multiple years of data and their careful attention to the value-added modeling strengthen the authors' claim for the robustness of their findings. Their results show strong implications that VAM teacher effect estimates serve as better indicators of teacher quality for both reading and math than observable teacher attributes such as qualifications and experience.

Daniel Aaronson and colleagues conducted a similar study using data from the Chicago Public Schools. Their data were restricted to one school district over 3 years. Their value-added model of teacher quality was the effect on 9th-grade math scores of a semester of instruction with a given teacher, controlling for 8th-grade math scores and student characteristics. They found that "the expected difference in math achievement between having an average teacher and one that is one standard deviation above average is educationally important."[151]

Another study conducted by economist Steven Rivkin and colleagues compared the relative contribution of teachers and schools to student achievement in Texas.[152] They concluded that schools are "by no means homogenous institutions" since they found substantial within-school heterogeneity in teacher quality. This variation in teacher quality, indicating that teachers have a powerful effect on reading and math achievement, was not explained by observable characteristics such as education (for example, having a master's degree) or experience. They further concluded that a one standard deviation improvement in teacher quality is of greater benefit than a "costly" 10-student reduction in class size. Jonah Rockoff, in a separate study of New Jersey panel data, also found large differences in quality among teachers within schools, and determined that a one-standard-deviation increase in teacher quality raised test scores by approximately 0.1 standard deviations in reading and math, a statistically significant but small effect.[153]

George Noell and Jeanne Burns used VAM to examine the comparative effectiveness of different teacher education programs in Louisiana.[154] The best predictors of student achievement were the students' prior test scores. Although they found some relationship between teacher preparation programs and teacher effectiveness, they concluded that there were too many doubts about other variables that should be included in the model and the questionable stability of the model across years to make definitive inferences.

Another study[155] used data from the Tennessee STAR project (where students and teachers were randomly assigned to classrooms in order to look at class-size effects).[156] The researchers' primary purpose in this study was to estimate the extent of unobservable K–12 teacher effects on student achievement, after controlling for student demographics, class size, and school fixed and random effects. They found that, consistent with previous studies, there were differences in teacher effectiveness. Their findings suggested that the difference in achievement gains between having a 25th-percentile teacher (a not-so-effective teacher) and a 75th-percentile teacher (an effective teacher) was over one-third of a standard deviation (0.35) in reading and almost half a standard deviation (0.48) in mathematics. Similarly, the difference in achievement gains between having a 50th-percentile teacher (an average teacher) and a 90th-percentile teacher (a very effective teacher) was about one-third of a standard deviation (0.33) in reading and somewhat smaller than half a standard deviation (0.46) in mathematics. In kindergarten, the effects were comparable, but somewhat larger for reading. Teacher effects were found to be more important than school effects, and more than observable teacher variables such as education and experience. Similar to previous studies, these differences between more and less effective teachers are still quite small but statistically significant. The evidence from this study, however, may be considered more persuasive because teachers and students were randomly assigned to classrooms. The authors also found that the teacher effects were greater in low-SES schools than in high-SES schools, implying that it matters more in low-SES schools which teacher a child receives than it does in high-SES schools. In sum, their findings have considerable policy implications for educators attempting to improve student achievement. Teacher selection and accountability appear to be more important than school choice or whole-school reform.

Teacher Effectiveness—Summary

From the accumulation of research on teacher effectiveness as a measure of teacher quality, we can begin to discern patterns in the evidence and clarity concerning the critical issues. The evidence is strong that teachers vary in effectiveness even within schools, and that students who are assigned teachers with a history of being more effective are likely to show greater achievement gains than those who are taught by historically less-effective teachers. It is also apparent that observable teacher variables such as education, credentials, paper qualifications, and experience are less reliable indicators of teacher quality than teacher effectiveness. What remains to be seen is whether it is possible to identify the factors that are most predictive of teacher effectiveness, and there needs to be clarity on the best and most reliable method for calculating value-added scores.

TEACHER QUALITY RESEARCH—ASSESSING THE EVIDENCE

In most areas of teacher quality research where attempts are made to determine which aspects of teacher quality are predictive of student learning, the findings are mixed. In mathematics, a teacher who has a mathematics degree or a license to teach mathematics appears more likely to have higher-achieving students, especially in the upper grades. For reading or language arts, the relationship does not hold. The evidence for other subject-specific degrees is lacking. Since many children practice reading or even learn to read outside of school, but mathematics knowledge is acquired primarily in the classroom, the teacher's qualifications may be more critical for math than for reading. The research on master's or other advanced degrees provides discouraging findings related to teacher quality and student achievement. Without the attendant focus on pedagogy, it appears that the mere accumulation of graduate degrees does not enable a teacher to translate that extra knowledge into useful classroom practice.

A teacher's level of experience makes the most difference during the early career years. Several studies demonstrate that a teacher's effectiveness climbs during the first 7 years or so before tapering off, and that by 10 years, experience ceases to be a factor. Inexperienced teachers tend to be clustered in the most challenging hard-to-staff schools, thus contributing to their typically below-average results.

A teacher's personal attributes may make a difference in certain situations. Students of the same race as their teacher may perform better, possibly because the teachers have higher expectations of students of the same race, and higher expectations may lead to greater achievement. The same may apply to gender. High expectations, however, may result from having higher-performing students, so the direction of the causality may be in doubt. The same is true for efficacy. The limited evidence that shows high feelings of efficacy are possibly linked to student achievement may result from the fact that teachers feel more efficacious because their students are high achievers rather than the other way around. Certain personal attributes, such as verbal ability, may be necessary but not sufficient conditions for effective teaching. Since many of the variables under the label of personal attributes are immutable, the findings are of limited practical use.

There is evidence that certain teaching practices are correlated with student achievement more than others. Typically, attempts to measure these practices through observation rely on standards-based instruments that demonstrate relatively low correlations with student test scores, making them of little use for high-stakes educational decisions. Information derived from the self-reports of teachers or students is even less reliable. Effective teaching practices may vary according to setting—grade level, subject matter, student demographics—complicating the effort to devise a measure that applies in all situations. It is possible, however, that there is a set of effective teaching practices that relates to all contexts.

A focus on teacher effectiveness as the main measure of teacher quality may hold the most promise for policy and educational decisions, and has certainly caught the attention of the Obama administration. With improved management of test databases, school districts are in better positions to determine how well teachers are contributing to student achievement gains. Journalists Jason Felch, Jason Song, and Doug Smith of the *Los Angeles Times* obtained the Los Angeles School District's 7-year database of student test scores linked to teachers and hired a statistician from the RAND Corporation to calculate value-added scores for all 3rd- through 5th-grade teachers, then published stories revealing how certain teachers raised student test scores and others had less positive results.[157] Their stated purpose was not to show up individual teachers but to challenge the school district to look at its own data and use the information to help improve the quality of its education. The authors' reports revealed important findings, many of which have been suggested by other research studies. They include:

- Students with teachers of the top 10% effectiveness performed 17 percentile points higher in English and 25 percentile points higher in math than students of teachers in the lowest 10% effectiveness group.
- Some students had the poorest-performing teachers for years in a row, severely limiting their chances at succeeding.
- The best teachers were not concentrated in the most affluent schools. Teacher effectiveness varied considerably within schools, and effective teachers were distributed across the school district.
- School effects were less important than teacher effects. Parents are better off choosing the right teacher than the right school.
- Experience, education, and training had little bearing on how much teachers raised their students' achievement.

The publication of these analyses attracted national attention and heated exchanges in the blogosphere. While some, including U.S. Secretary of Education Arne Duncan, welcomed the exposé, others felt that it was premature to name teachers when there is still no agreement on the best way to calculate value-added scores and there is considerable variation in results among the existing methods.

Most of the teacher effectiveness studies involve the calculation of value-added scores using standardized test data. Apart from the issues of how best to calculate these scores, there is some question as to whether standardized tests are the best way to measure student learning when they do not necessarily assess the knowledge directly associated with the state standards and curriculum, which are the focus of instruction. In short, standardized tests often fail to measure much of what is learned in the classroom, and take no account of students' motivation to learn or their creativity. Even statisticians who calculate value-added scores warn that they are more reliable as estimates of a school's effectiveness than of a teacher's. Also, it is difficult to control the variation in learning gains and losses that may go on during the summer vacation. These are likely to be captured to some extent by controls for parent education level and poverty status, but not entirely. Another factor that may have bearing on the value-added issue is research that children's learning does not always occur in a straight line. Nicole McNeil, a psychologist at the University of Notre Dame, tested whether children's ability to solve mathematics equivalence problems increased as a function of age.[158] She found after two experiments that children between the ages of about 7 and 10 actually get worse before they get better, showing a clear U-shaped learning curve. This phenomenon would have implications for the calculation of a teacher's value-added scores, depending on where the class falls in the learning cycle.

We must conclude from the research that we do not know with any degree of certainty which of the variables that have been postulated as representing teacher quality are the most important for student learning. The many studies that have found positive relationships do not provide us with definitive answers about teacher quality. Some refer to schools rather than teachers, others work from too small a database, and others investigate too many predictors so that we cannot conclude which factors are the most critical. What we do know is that teachers make a difference, and students benefit most from having effective teachers. There have been many attempts to determine what effective teachers do and how to measure it. In the next chapter, we will examine some of those attempts in more detail, and see exactly how well they predict teacher effectiveness.

4

Measuring Teacher Quality

How you measure teacher quality will depend on your definition of quality, which itself is a function of your educational perspective and your purpose for identifying quality teachers in the first place. We may take the information reviewed in the previous chapters to construct the following general-purpose working definition of teacher quality: The set of teacher qualifications, knowledge, experience, personal attributes, and pedagogical practices that result in positive student outcomes. The student outcomes typically measured are performance on achievement tests, but may be expanded to include the development of thinking skills and creativity, life skills, and preparation for work, among others. While a teacher's formal qualifications, knowledge, and personal attributes have been shown to have some relation to student achievement under some circumstances, they all serve as potential predictors of how well a teacher will perform in the classroom, i.e., teach. It is what the teacher does in the classroom that leads to student learning, and a teacher's practice is influenced to a greater or lesser degree by his or her knowledge, training, and personal characteristics. The teacher's types of licensure, degrees, verbal abilities, and so on serve at the most as necessary rather than sufficient conditions for student learning. One may argue, therefore, that a teacher's classroom practice should be the primary focus for the assessment of quality, since all the other factors are reflected in the way they teach.

On the basis of this rationale, we will examine those kinds of assessment that focus on classroom practice as an indirect measure of effectiveness, and effectiveness itself, as measured by student achievement on standardized tests. At present, most assessments are based on teaching standards, such as those devised by the National Council for Accreditation of Teacher Education (NCATE),[1] and the National Board for Professional Teaching Standards (NBPTS),[2] and education boards in many states.[3] Typically, these standards are vague, necessarily so because there is no common curriculum or other educational infrastructure with which to align them.[4] To some extent, the standards reflect findings from the so-called process-product studies of the 1960s and 1970s that examined what teachers did to improve student learning. Jere Brophy and Tom Good summarized the results of these studies in various articles in the mid-1980s.[5] The studies related the classroom practices to year-end achievement scores, not achievement *gains*, so they do not connect quality with effectiveness, as it is now commonly defined. They examined both teaching time on task and the quality of teaching. The findings indicated that students achieved more when their teachers emphasized academic objectives in establishing expectations and allocating time, used effective management strategies to ensure that academic learning time was maximized, paced students through the curriculum briskly but in small steps, and adapted curriculum materials based on their knowledge of students' characteristics. Teachers differed in how they performed instructional behaviors such as giving information, asking questions, and providing feedback. Homework was an important factor, and the effects of certain practices were context-specific (i.e., to grade level or subject matter). The conclusion from these reviews was that any attempt to improve student achievement should be based on the development of effective teaching behavior. Subsequently, process-product research has been criticized for focusing solely on routine activities and basic skills, rather than on higher-order thinking or understanding.[6] Reform-minded teaching movements promoted by NBPTS and the Carnegie Corporation looked to develop more sophisticated and more rigorous teaching standards than those reflected in the process-product studies.[7] David Cohen opines that these attempts faced the insurmountable difficulty of attempting to work "within a nonsystem that contained none of the infrastructure that could support such an enterprise."[8]

Information on what teachers do in the classroom may be collected in a number of different ways. We have already discussed research that used classroom observation techniques, teacher self-reports, student reports, and principal evaluations. Other sources of data may include teacher portfolios and other artifacts such as lesson plans and student work. We will discuss each of these assessment methods in the following sections.

CLASSROOM OBSERVATION

Of the many forms that observation instruments may take, only a few have been extensively researched. Instruments vary in length, focus, how often they are administered, who does the rating, whether they are specific to subject matter or education level, and the thoroughness of the training. An observation instrument may have a particular purpose: formative or summative, formal or informal, high-stakes or low-stakes. A good observation instrument is both valid and reliable. Validity refers to the extent to which the instrument measures what it professes to measure and that what it measures reflects the aspects of classroom behavior that professionals agree (or scientific evidence shows) are important for student learning. An instrument may be valid for one purpose (say, for determining the need for professional development) but not for another (say, for hiring or firing).[9] Reliability concerns whether different judges arrive at the same rating, and whether ratings are consistent over time and in different settings. Assessments based on observation are subject to the biases of the observer, as well as the cognitive demands of the task, both of which factors are apt to affect reliability. Many classroom observation instruments have been developed.[10] We will examine the few that have attendant research related to connections with student achievement.

Charlotte Danielson's Framework for Teaching

As we saw in the previous chapter in the section titled "Studies Based on Classroom Observation," the most widely used and best-known observation protocol is probably Charlotte Danielson's Framework for Teaching, originally published in 1996 and revised in 2007. The Framework consists of four domains of teaching based on the *Praxis III*[11] criteria developed at ETS when Danielson was part of the *Praxis III* development team. The Framework's four domains are: planning and preparation, classroom environment, instruction, and professional responsibilities. They are broken into 22 components, each of which is further subdivided into elements. Each of the 76 total elements is evaluated on a 4-point scale from *unsatisfactory*, through *basic* and *proficient*, to *distinguished*. The primary stated purpose of the Framework is for formative feedback to teachers, but the manual lists a number of different uses: preparation of new teachers, recruitment and hiring of teachers, a road map for novices, guidance for experienced professionals, a structure for focusing improvement efforts, and communication with the larger community. On the back cover is listed a further use, that of "teacher evaluation processes."

The Framework bills itself as research-based, aligned to the INTASC teaching standards (see Chapter 1), and grounded in a "constructionist view" of teaching and learning.[12] Its items are constructed around four teaching domains: 1) Planning and Preparation; 2) The Classroom Environment; 3) Instruction; 4) Professional Responsibilities. Over the years, there have been several research studies looking at the correlation between scores on the Framework and student achievement gains. Over the period from 2009 to 2011, the Framework was one of the teacher evaluation instruments under scrutiny by researchers funded by the Bill and Melinda Gates Foundation "Measures of Effective Teaching" (MET) project to determine evaluation measures of teaching that are the best predictors of student learning.[13]

In the previous chapter, we referred to the studies conducted at school districts in various parts of the country: Coventry, Rhode Island; Los Angeles; Reno, Nevada; and Cincinnati. In general, these studies showed at best small to moderate correlations between scores on the *Framework* and student achievement gains. The correlations varied in size and significance according to grade level and subject matter, perhaps as a result of differences among the sites in the modifications to the instrument, the training of the raters, who did the ratings, and the number of observations performed. Herbert Heneman and colleagues reviewed these studies and produced a matrix (from which Table 4.1 is adapted) to summarize their characteristics across the different sites.[14]

A more recent attempt to relate a modified form of Danielson's Framework to student achievement was in a study by Tom Kane and colleagues using later observations of classrooms in the Cincinnati schools than those previously conducted and referred to above.[15] Their database consisted of more than 2,000 teacher evaluations over the years from 2000 to 2009. Most of the teachers were observed between two and six times. From the district records, they calculated average scores on the teacher evaluations and value-added scores for the teachers. They looked for information on whether classroom-based measures of teaching quality were related to student growth and on which types of practice were most effective at raising student achievement. They found that an overall move from one basic level to the next on the Danielson scale (for example, from "basic" to "proficient" or from "proficient" to "distinguished") was associated with about one-sixth of a standard deviation of student achievement gain, the strongest association thus far in such studies, but still quite small. They further found that high scores on all "teaching practice" and "classroom environment" skills are correlated with student achievement gains. Also, where teachers scored equally across all domains, improvement in classroom management (domain 2) is likely to generate achievement gains. Last, for teachers with equal ratings on the "routinized content and standards focused teaching" element, those utilizing "questioning and discussion" practices will generate higher achievement in reading but not in math.

It must be stressed, however, that these relatively weak associations are based on more than classroom observations; to arrive at evaluations of particular teachers a full assessment must be made across the four domains described by Danielson, which in addition to frequent observations of classroom practice depend on artifacts such as lesson plans and samples of student work. Consequently, the evidence suggests that observations *may* be one of several inputs that contribute to a rich, intensive, and slightly predictive measure of teacher performance, but this relationship has not been demonstrated for observations alone.

With the evidence available so far, we may conclude that the Framework is a useful measure of teacher quality, particularly for formative purposes. Since it is designed for all subjects and grade levels, it may suffer from being too general and insensitive to the particular nuances of quality teaching for different subjects and different grade levels. Most of the research involved applications of some "modified" version of the Framework, implying a flexibility but, at the same time, not indicating whether it functions with equal results across all incarnations.

Table 4.1. Summary of Evaluation Systems Based on the Danielson FRAMEWORK in Place at Four Sites

	District Background	Teachers	Schools	Pilot Test Year	Year First Full Implementation	Competency Model (Evaluation Standards)	Evaluation Procedures	Evaluators
Cincinnati	Midwest, urban 40,000 students, primarily African American	2,500	81	1999–2000	2000–2001	Customized version of Framework for Teaching; 4 domains, 16 standards	Comprehensive evaluation on all domains for new teachers and veterans identified as needing improvement, at certain steps on the schedule, or desiring to become lead teachers. Original plan was for comprehensive evaluation once every 5 years. All others undergo less rigorous annual evaluation on one domain each year. Comprehensive evaluation consisted of 5–6 classroom observations and a teacher-prepared portfolio.	Peer evaluators, principals, and assistant principals
Reno	Western, urban-suburban-rural 60,000 students, majority White, large Hispanic minority	3,300	88	1999–2000	2000–2001	Minor modifications to Framework for Teaching; 4 domains, 23 components, 68 elements	Non-tenured teachers evaluated on all domains/elements via 9 classroom observations. Tenured teachers evaluated on 1 domain (minor) or 2 domains (major) over 3-year cycle via at least 1 classroom observation. No portfolio required, but evaluators also look at artifacts like student work.	Principals and assistant principals

Country								
Coventry	East coast, suburban 6,000 students, predominantly White	475	9	N/A	1998–1999	Modified version of Framework for Teaching; 3 domains, 18 components, 56 elements	Non-tenured teachers evaluated on a subset of the standards each year for 2 years, then receive a full evaluation in the 3rd year. Evaluation is based on at least 2 observations. Tenured teachers are evaluated on all domains every 2, 3, or 4 years depending on prior rating level. At least 1 observation is required.	Principals and department heads
Los Angeles	West coast, urban 1,200 student, predominantly Hispanic	40 pre-K through 5	1 charter school	1999–2000	2000–2001	2 domains modeled on Danielson Framework; 12 other content-specific domains developed locally	All teachers evaluated annually, with 2 ratings per year on selected domains, primarily via classroom observations. Observations are conducted as many times as is necessary over a 2-week period each semester. No portfolio is required, but evaluators also look at artifacts like student work. All rated on 5 core domains and selected content-relevant domains.	Self, peer, and assistant principals

The Classroom Assessment Scoring System (CLASS)

Based on theories of child development, CLASS[16] is an instrument constructed originally by Robert Pianta and colleagues at the University of Virginia to look at teaching in early childhood education contexts. CLASS focuses on teacher-student interactions, and consists of 10 dimensions across three domains that cover *emotional support* (positive and negative classroom climate, teacher sensitivity, regard for student perspectives), *classroom organization* (behavior management, productivity, instructional learning formats), and *instructional support* (concept development, quality of feedback, language modeling), together with a fourth domain, *student engagement*. They are displayed in Table 4.2. Each dimension is rated on a 7-point scale ranging from 1–2 (low), 3–5 (midrange), and 6–7 (high). A factor analysis of CLASS yielded two factors, *Emotional Climate* and *Instructional Climate*.[17] Emotional climate is a composite of the items related to Positive Climate, Negative Climate (reversed), and Behavior Management. Instructional Climate is a composite of the items related to Productivity, Concept Development, Instructional Learning Format, and Quality of Feedback. The CLASS instrument is organized with student engagement as the dependent variable, and is believed to measure the effectiveness of teachers. One version is designed for preschoolers, and another for children in kindergarten through grade 5. A third version was developed for middle school grades. The measure requires trained raters to conduct at least four 20-minute cycles of observation in target classrooms. Training requires raters to achieve scores the same as or within one point of those produced by master raters on a set of five consensus-scored 20-minute training clips.

A small number of studies have looked at the correlation between CLASS scores and student achievement and social growth, mostly in preschool or the earliest grades. One study was conducted by the developers of the instrument using two scales from a precursor to CLASS, the Classroom Observation System for First Grade (COS-1).[18] In this study, 910 5- to 6-year-old children who were part of an NICHD Study of Early Child Care were followed over 1 year.[19] Some of the children were identified as demographically "at-risk" (n = 249) and some were deemed as functionally "at-risk" (n = 99). Demographically at-risk was defined as having a mother with less than a 4-year college degree. Functionally at-risk required a child to score beyond a cut point on at least two of four factors: sustained attention, externalizing behavior, social skills, and academic competence. Those having 1st-grade teachers with high ratings for instructional and emotional support demonstrated achievement scores and student-teacher relationships that were no different from those of their low-risk peers. Those in less supportive classrooms ranked lower on both outcomes. Although the differences were statistically significant, the effect sizes were quite small.

Later studies used the CLASS instrument itself. One group of researchers, including Pianta and colleagues, looked at classroom quality in preschool.[20] Among

Table 4.2. Ten Dimensions and Three Domains of the Classroom Assessment Scoring System

Emotional Support	Classroom Organization	Instructional Support
Positive Climate Reflects the overall emotional tone of the classroom and the connection between the teacher and students. *Negative Climate* Reflects the overall level of expressed negativity in the classroom. *Teacher Sensitivity* Reflects the teacher's responsiveness to children's needs and awareness of students' level of academic and emotional functioning. *Regard for Student Perspectives* Reflects the degree to which the teacher's interactions with students and classroom activities place an emphasis on students' interests, motivations, and points of view.	*Behavior Management* Reflects the teacher's ability to use effective methods to prevent and redirect misbehavior. *Productivity* Reflects how well the teacher manages instructional time and routines so that students have an opportunity to learn. *Instructional Learning Formats* Reflects what the teacher does either during the lesson or in providing activities, centers, and materials to maximize students' engagement and ability to learn.	*Concept Development* Reflects the teacher's use of instructional discussions and activities to promote students' higher-order thinking skills and cognition. *Quality of Feedback* Reflects the degree to which the teacher's provision of feedback is focused on expanding learning and understanding. *Language Modeling* Reflects the quality and amount of the teacher's use of language stimulation and facilitation techniques during individual, small-group, and large-group interactions with children.

Note: The fourth domain is Student Engagement.

the predictors of academic and social skills were the two CLASS dimensions of emotional and instructional support. The measure of instructional support was statistically significantly correlated with all the academic outcomes (vocabulary, oral expression, rhyming, applied problems, and letter naming).

Another study of some 3,000 pre-kindergarten students randomly selected from about 700 state-funded pre-kindergarten classrooms (also randomly selected) measured scores on CLASS against academic outcomes. There were small significant correlations between Instructional Climate and the literacy outcomes of vocabulary and expressive language.[21]

Other work with CLASS has focused on validity (including one for Finnish kindergartens) or on relationships other than student academic learning.[22] Studies have yet to be published on the use of the version targeting the upper grades. CLASS is also one of the instruments being examined as part of the Gates' MET study. Because of its origin in developmental psychology, only one domain of CLASS is specific to instructional issues, potentially limiting its ability to be highly predictive of academic achievement. Also, the extensive training necessary for achieving and maintaining rating reliability makes it somewhat impractical for use outside research settings.

The Protocol for Language Arts Teaching Observation (PLATO)

PLATO is a recently developed classroom observation protocol focused on middle and high school English Language Arts (ELA) instruction that was developed as part of a research study on classroom practices by Pam Grossman and colleagues at the Center to Support Excellence in Teaching (CSET) at Stanford University.[23] At the time of writing, it is still undergoing refinement after an initial pilot study.[24] The specific aim of the study was to discover more effective teacher practices as measured by their impact on student achievement. The authors constructed PLATO with reference to the existing literature on effective instruction in secondary level English/language arts. The pilot version of the instrument included 13 elements that encompass a number of key areas of ELA classroom instruction together with a scoring rubric with a 4-point scale. The elements are intended to measure distinct aspects of classroom instruction that operate independently of one another. The Web site states that:

> The tool enables observers to zero in on specific dimensions of quality teaching, such as: quality of classroom discussion, the level of intellectual challenge provided to students, and accommodations for English learners.

The elements in the draft version were:

- *Purpose* (focuses on the expressed clarity of ELA objectives, both in the short and long term)
- *Representation of Content* (captures the effectiveness of the teacher's explanations and examples in addition to evidence of his or her content knowledge)
- *Connections to Prior Knowledge* (measures the extent to which new material is connected to students' previous academic knowledge)
- *Connections to Personal and Cultural Experience* (focuses on the extent to which new material is connected to students' personal and cultural experiences)

- *Models* (captures the availability of exemplars to guide student work)
- *Explicit Strategy Instruction* (measures the teacher's ability to teach ELA strategies that can be used flexibly and independently)
- *Guided Practice* (focuses on structured and scaffolded opportunities for students to practice ELA skills, concepts, or strategies)
- *Classroom Discourse* (reflects the opportunity for and quality of student conversations with the teacher and among peers)
- *Text-Based Instruction* (focuses on how grounded English/language arts instruction is in a variety of texts)
- *Accommodations for Language Learning* (captures the range of strategies and supports a teacher might use to make a lesson accessible to non-native English speakers and native English speakers struggling to develop ELA skills)
- *Behavior Management* (focuses on the degree to which behavior management facilitates academic work)
- *Time Management* (focuses on how well paced and efficient tasks and transitions are in the classroom).

The instrument is administered in 15-minute time samples of classroom activity. Approximately two PLATO cycles can be captured for every 45-minute class period. Observers also code for the content being taught during the segment and various aspects of student participation. PLATO's developers have clearly benefited from exposure to the CLASS instrument described in the previous section.

In the pilot study that looked at the connection between PLATO scores and value-added gains, researchers estimated value-added scores using two different formulas for a tiny sample of 24 New York City 6th- to 8th-grade teachers in the 3rd to 5th years of their careers. They grouped teachers into quartiles according to their value-added performances and created 12 matched pairs, each with one teacher from the high-performing 4th quartile and one from the moderate-performing 2nd quartile. Teachers were observed on 6 separate days by trained raters of PLATO. Teachers were also rated on some elements of the CLASS protocol. A second observer took field notes, and teacher logs and student assignments were collected. The only element of PLATO that statistically significantly differentiated between teachers in the two groups was Explicit Strategy Instruction. The authors concluded that high-quartile teachers "had a different profile of instructional practices" from the low-quartile teachers. Apart from the relationship reflected in this rather general statement, the researchers were not able to draw any more concrete conclusions about the ability of PLATO to distinguish the more from the less effective teachers, as defined by their value-added scores. They acknowledge that even the element of Explicit Strategy Instruction occurs rarely, and the mean scores for this element were the lowest of all elements except for English Language

Learner (ELL) accommodations. PLATO, they admit, is "far from perfect." As a result, they report having revised the instrument and:

> developed broader instructional factors within PLATO, collapsing, disaggregating, and eliminating elements that are highly correlated with one another, and changed the scoring from a 7 point to a 4 point scale.[25]

They refer to a follow-up study using the revised version with 177 New York City middle school teachers. We await the results.

Mathematical Quality of Instruction (MQI)

A third instrument under testing in the Gates MET study, the Mathematical Quality of Instruction (MQI), was developed by a group of researchers inspired by the work of Deborah Ball and colleagues at the University of Michigan. The initial focus of their work was to document and measure teachers' mathematical knowledge for teaching (MKT), a construct that "includes both the mathematical knowledge that is common to individuals working in diverse professions and the mathematical knowledge that is specialized to teaching."[26] The MQI is definitely a tool for researchers rather than for administrators or evaluators in the field. The technical manual (published in 2006, so it may be out of date) refers to 83 codes grouped into five sections, and an accompanying glossary that provides overall instructions and details on each code.[27] The five sections are:

Section I: Instructional formats and content
Section II: Knowledge of mathematical terrain of enacted lesson
Section III: Use of mathematics with students
Section IV: Mathematical features of the curriculum and
    the teacher's guide
Section V: Use of mathematics to teach equitably

A subsequent publication clusters the codes into the scales listed in Table 4.3 "in order to compress data for presentation, and because we were measuring an underlying or latent trait."[28]

A small set of five case studies indicates a strong association (from 0.30 to 0.86) between MKT and MQI, but no evidence of any effect on student performance.

At a presentation at the annual conference of the American Educational Research Association, Heather Hill and colleagues reported on an examination of the link between MQI scores and teacher value-added estimates.[29] They collected value-added data on 250 middle school math teachers and derived overall MQI scores for teachers using a 3-point Likert scale in which "low" represented a lesson

Table 4.3. Elements of the Mathematical Quality of Instruction (MQI)

Element	Description
Mathematics Errors	The presence of computational, linguistic, representational, or other mathematical errors in instruction; contains subcategory specifically for errors with mathematical language
Responding to Students Inappropriately	The degree to which teacher either misinterprets or, in the case of student misunderstanding, fails to respond to student utterance
Connecting Classroom Practice to Mathematics	The degree to which classroom practice is connected to important and worthwhile mathematical ideas and procedures as opposed to either non-mathematical focus, such as classroom management, or activities that do not require mathematical thinking, such as students following directions to cut, color, and paste, but with no obvious connections between these activities and mathematical meaning(s)
Richness of the Mathematics	The use of multiple representations, linking among representations, mathematical explanation and justification, and explicitness around mathematical practices such as proof and reasoning
Responding to Students Appropriately	The degree to which teacher can correctly interpret students' mathematical utterances and address student misunderstandings
Mathematical language	The density of accurate mathematical language in instruction, the use of language to clearly convey mathematical ideas, as well as any explicit discussion of the use of mathematical language

with significant teacher mathematical errors; "medium" corresponded to lessons with fewer errors, yet mostly routine instruction; and "high" was reserved for lessons with no errors as well as significant mathematical richness through explanation, representations, and strong interactions with students. They reported some correlations between value-added scores and MQI ratings, but some teachers had much higher value-added scores than their low MQI scores would have predicted. These data had not yet been published at the time of writing and should be considered preliminary. We await the results of the MET study for a definitive estimate of the predictability of the MQI for student achievement.

Teaching Standards and Performance Rubrics

Often, researchers or program leaders will devise a rubric based on a set of teaching standards in order to evaluate teaching practice for formative or summative purposes. One example was devised by John Shachter and Yeow Meng Thum for the Milken Family Foundation.[30] They identified and developed six standards from a review of past research: Questions, Feedback, Presentation, Lesson Structure and Pacing, Lesson Objectives, and Classroom Environment. From the research on how students learned and on effective teaching strategies, they developed five further standards: Grouping Students, Thinking, Activities, Motivating Students, and Teacher Knowledge of Students. From the research on teacher qualifications, they added one standard related to Content Knowledge. An abridged description of the rubric may be found in Table 4.4.

Schacter and Thum conducted one study using their rubric and concluded that it was "highly predictive of student academic progress across the elementary grades." Their sample consisted of 52 volunteer teachers from five Arizona elementary schools. Each teacher was observed eight times over 1 school year, some scheduled and some unscheduled, at different times of day. Graduate students were trained to use the rubric using five training tapes until inter-rater reliability was acceptable. Either two or three researchers observed a subsample of eight teachers. Pre- and post-scores on the Stanford 9 Achievement Tests Reading, Language, and Mathematics total scores served as the outcome measures. Through multilevel modeling, they controlled for classroom composition and student demographics. They found that teachers who implemented effective teaching as measured by the rubric produced students who made significant gains such that one standard deviation increase in Teaching Quality translated into increased classroom achievement gains of 6.80 points in language, 7.06 points in mathematics, and 4.73 points in reading. It is unlikely that a rubric such as theirs would be adopted widely by school administrators, however, given the high training demands and the need for as many as eight classroom visits per teacher.

Summary

As Dan Goldhaber and Emily Anthony have stated, perhaps the only way to measure teacher effectiveness is "through direct observations of their teaching."[31] Certainly, there are several advantages to conducting classroom observations. First, observation protocols may be designed to focus on any of a number of aspects of teaching and so may be targeted to the specific interests of the observer. They may be used for formative or summative purposes, and, if developed and used

Table 4.4. Teaching Standards and Performance Rubrics for Quality Teaching Measure used by John Schacter and Yeow Meng Thum (Abridged)

Variable	Exemplary (5)	Proficient (3)	Ineffective (1)
Teacher Content Knowledge	Teacher displays extensive content knowledge of all the subjects he or she teaches.	Teacher displays accurate content knowledge of all the subjects he or she teaches.	Teacher displays underdeveloped content knowledge in several subject areas.
Lesson Objectives	All learning objectives are explicitly communicated.	Most learning objectives are communicated.	Few learning objectives are communicated .
Presentation	Presentation always includes: visuals ... examples ... modeling ... concise communication ... logical sequencing ... no irrelevant information.	Mostly includes: visuals ... examples ... modeling ... concise communication ... logical sequencing ... no irrelevant information.	Rarely includes: visuals ... examples ... modeling ... concise communication ... logical sequencing ... no irrelevant information.
Lesson Structure and Pacing	Teacher optimizes instructional time, teaches more material, and demands better performance from every student.	Most lessons start promptly.	Lesson has structure but may be missing closure or introductory elements during transitions.

(continued)

Table 4.4. (continued)

Variable	Exemplary (5)	Proficient (3)	Ineffective (1)
Activities	Activities always support lesson objectives; are challenging; sustain 90% of the students' attention; provide time for reflection; are relevant to students' lives; … provide frequent opportunities for [peer] interaction]; induce … curiosity … provide … choices … incorporate multimedia … or manipulatives.	Activities [mostly] support lesson objectives; are sometimes challenging; sustain 75% attention; are sometimes relevant to students' lives; provide some opportunities for [peer] interaction; sometimes incorporate multimedia … or manipulatives	Activities: rarely support lesson objectives; are rarely challenging; sustain less than 50% … attention; are rarely relevant…; provide few opportunities for [peer] interaction; rarely incorporate multimedia … or manipulatives
Questions	Teacher questions are varied providing a balanced mix of question types.	Teacher questions include some question types.	Teacher questions include few question types
Feedback	Feedback makes students explicitly aware of performance criteria in the form of rubrics or criterion charts.	Feedback sometimes makes students aware of performance criteria.	Quality and timeliness of feedback is inconsistent…

Table 4.4. (continued)

Variable	Exemplary (5)	Proficient (3)	Ineffective (1)
Grouping Students	The instructional grouping arrangements (either whole class, small groups, pairs, individual; hetero- or homogenous ability) consistently maximize student understanding and learning efficiency.	The instructional grouping arrangements (either whole class, small groups, pairs, individual; hetero- or homogenous ability) adequately maximize student understanding and learning efficiency.	The instructional grouping arrangements (either whole class, small groups, pairs, individual; hetero- or homogenous ability) inhibit student understanding and learning efficiency.
Thinking	Over the course of multiple observations, the teacher consistently and thoroughly teaches all four types of thinking]: [analytical, . . . practical, . . . creative, . . . and research-based] .	Over the course of multiple observations, the teacher consistently and thoroughly teaches two types of thinking.	Teacher implements few learning experiences that thoroughly teach any type of thinking.
Motivating Students	The teacher consistently organizes the content so that it is personally meaningful and relevant to students.	The teacher sometimes organizes the content so that it is meaningful to students.	Teacher rarely organizes content so that it is personally meaningful to students.

(continued)

Table 4.4. (continued)

Variable	Exemplary (5)	Proficient (3)	Ineffective (1)
Environment	Students are consistently well-behaved and on task.	Students are mostly well-behaved and on task with possible minor interruptions.	Students not well-behaved and often off task.
Teacher Knowledge of Students	Teacher practices display understanding of student anticipated learning difficulties . . . [and] incorporate student interests and cultural heritage . . . [and] provides differentiated instruction	Teacher practices display understanding of some student learning difficulties, . . . sometimes incorporate student interests and cultural heritage . . . [and] sometimes provides differentiated instruction	Teacher practices display minimal knowledge of student anticipated learning difficulties, . . . rarely incorporate student interests and cultural heritage . . . [and teacher provides] little differentiated instruction

scientifically, can avoid many of the biases that come with self-report data. Observations based on video recordings of lessons have the benefit that ratings may be conducted by several judges, thus strengthening reliability. On the minus side, many observation instruments developed by researchers have not been validated in the field and are possibly too cumbersome for anyone besides the developers themselves to use. The more training and calibration for reliability that is needed, the less chance an instrument will be of practical use to the educators who are most likely to need it. Most reports of reliability estimates show agreements around 0.80, indicating a 20% rate of disagreement. Is this too much? Also, raters are frequently considered to be in agreement when they are within 1 point of one another or of the master rating for calibration purposes. One may argue that it is a somewhat lax standard if raters can be 2 points apart on a 7-point scale and still be considered to be in agreement.

Further, as we have seen, most observation instruments are designed to measure performance on a set of teaching standards and are only tested for their ability to predict student learning after the fact. For those instruments that have been linked to value-added scores, the correlations are mostly too low for them to form the basis for any high-stakes decisions. An instrument that starts with items of proven ability to predict student learning gains has yet to be developed. Another challenge of observation instruments stems from their inherent flexibility, or lack thereof. An instrument designed to measure the quality of mathematics teaching, for example, may not be appropriate for evaluating reading lessons. A generic measure, on the other hand, may fail to assess the quality of teaching strategies that are specific to a given content area.

EVALUATIONS BY SCHOOL ADMINISTRATORS

Unrestricted by the confines of an ivory tower, principals and vice principals use various methods, including classroom observations, to evaluate teachers, usually for summative purposes.[32] Unlike most researchers, principals have access to a great deal of information about their teachers beyond that collected from classroom visits. They receive feedback from students and parents, they can look at previous test scores and other student work products, they may learn historical information about teachers from previous principals, and they may interact with the teachers outside of the classroom.

Evaluation by a school administrator can range from one or more quick visits or walkthroughs[33] to a formal observation using an instrument such as the Danielson Framework or a rubric, accompanied or not by interviews and reviews of work products and test scores. We will address more thoroughly the question of a principal's ability to identify quality teaching in the next chapter. For the moment, it is enough to know that school administrators do quick visits more often than full formal observations using an established protocol, and rarely undergo the training necessary to use such instruments reliably.[34]

Several researchers have studied the predictive qualities of principal evaluations. Earlier studies support the findings from the literature on supervisor ratings in general, in which, at best, a weak relationship is recorded between subjective ratings and objective performance.[35] Supervisors are frequently open to influence from non-performance factors that have to do with the personal characteristics of the subordinate in relation to the supervisor. In one study of vocational/rehabilitation counselors, for example, no relationship was found between the subjective and objective measures. The subjective measures were more a reflection of the quality of the interpersonal relationship between the supervisor and subordinate.[36]

Richard Murnane studied elementary teachers in Connecticut using a cross-sectional analysis. He found teacher evaluations were predictive of student achievement, but only to a "modest" degree.[37,38] A cross-sectional analysis of test-score levels has the disadvantages of not accounting for the effects of other educational inputs, particularly past teachers, on current performance, and precludes the use of fixed or random effects estimators to control for unobserved differences in student factors.[39] Other studies showed small correlations between principal evaluations and student achievement. Donald Medley and Homer Coker summarized these studies as showing that the evaluations are only "slightly more accurate than if they were based on pure chance."[40]

In a recent study, Brian Jacob and Lars Lefgren attempted to eliminate some of the deficiencies they noted in the earlier research. They asked 13 elementary principals in one school district to rate all their 200 or so teachers on a 10-point scale across a variety of dimensions.[41] One of the dimensions was "the ability to raise student math (or reading) achievement." They calculated value-added scores for each teacher and compared the subjective principal ratings with the standardized gain scores. After adjusting for estimation error, they showed correlations of 0.29 for reading and 0.32 for math. While these correlations reach statistical significance at the 0.05 level, they are too low to be of any use in making any educational decisions with regard to these teachers. When asked to identify teachers in the top or bottom categories of raising student achievement, principals were correct about 55% of the time in reading and 70% of the time in math compared with the corresponding probabilities of 14% and 26% that would be expected if ratings were randomly assigned to teachers. Principals were not successful, however, in identifying teachers in the middle of the distribution. Jacob and Lefgren conclude that their findings provide "compelling evidence that good teaching is, at least to some extent, observable by those close to the education process."[42] I think this statement should be qualified to reflect the fact that the principals are likely to arrive at their evaluations by appealing to more than the "observable" evidence obtained from classroom visits, including what they may know from a teacher's history of student achievement scores and other information about their performance. Even then, they are only between 55% and 70% accurate at identifying the highest- and lowest-performing teachers. Furthermore, Douglas Harris makes the point that since principals consider factors other than student achievement in making their confidential assessments, we would not expect their evaluations to equal teacher value-added scores.[43]

Doug Harris and Tim Sass interviewed 30 Florida principals about their elementary, middle, and high school teachers, asking them for overall ratings of effectiveness, and ratings on the following characteristics: caring, communication skills, enthusiasm, intelligence, knowledge of subject, strong teaching skills, motivation, works well with grade team/department, works well with me (the principal), contributes to school activities beyond the classroom, and contributes to overall school community. These characteristics were based on previous research to determine what was most important to principals when conducting hiring interviews. No ratings were based specifically on classroom observation, although most of the principals probably would have at least done walkthroughs. The researchers found a statistically significant positive correlation between principals' overall ratings and value-added achievement scores. However, the relationship between the subjective and objective assessments was not perfect. Although there was a relatively high correlation between a principal's estimation of a teacher's ability to raise student achievement in math and actual math value-added scores, the relationship between the equivalent question and reading scores was insignificant. The authors concluded that, although principal evaluations are better predictors of student achievement than other indicators (such as education and experience), they are not strong enough to form the basis for making high-stakes decisions.[44]

David Wilkerson and colleagues compared principal evaluations with other methods of teacher assessment for the prediction of student gains in mathematics, reading, and English/ language arts. Their sample comprised 35 K–12 teachers and four principals in a small Wyoming school district that had adopted an evaluation process known as the 360° feedback appraisal whereby data are collected from superiors, subordinates, peers, and customers (in a business setting). In this instance, the principal evaluations were not good predictors of student learning.[45]

There is some evidence that when they are not operating under research conditions, principals are frequently overly lenient in their evaluations, so that most teachers end up with better than satisfactory ratings. A recent study of 36,000 teacher evaluations conducted in Chicago between 2003 and 2006 found that 93% of Chicago teachers earned the two highest ratings ("superior" or "excellent"), and only 3 in 1,000 received "unsatisfactory" ratings. Even in 87 schools that had been identified as failing, 79% did not award a single unsatisfactory rating to teachers between 2003 and 2005. When questioned, the majority of veteran principals in the district admitted to inflating performance ratings for some of their teachers.[46]

Summary

In summary, the research is mixed regarding principal accuracy in predicting teacher performance, as measured by the standardized test–score results of their students. The most recent research suggests that principal evaluations are most accurate at the top and bottom ends of the teacher performance range, but even then it is doubtful that they are strong enough for any high-stakes decisions. Both teacher evaluations and value-added scores are better assessments of teacher effectiveness than other variables such as degrees, experience, and type of licensure. It is often recommended that the best evaluations of effectiveness might be a combination of value-added scores and principal evaluations. It is not clear what weight should be given to principal evaluations in making high-stakes decisions, such as for compensation and firing. To overcome the common problem of inflation in principal assessments, it may be necessary to increase principals' training to do observations, their use of valid instruments, and to require calibration for reliability.

TEACHER PORTFOLIOS

In some settings, teachers are required to assemble materials that demonstrate evidence of their teaching practice, their contributions to the life of the school, and their students' progress. Portfolios might include items such as lesson plans, homework assignments, quizzes, and other assessments; samples of student work; lesson videos; teacher notes; and parent communications. Teachers-in-training are often required to put together portfolios as part of the licensure process and some states have adopted the construction of portfolios for the assessment of experienced teachers. One well-known example of a program that uses portfolios with teachers post-training is the Beginning Educator Support and Training Program (BEST) from the state of Connecticut.

Perhaps the best-known use of portfolios is by the certification program of the National Board for Professional Teaching Standards (NBPTS). Teachers apply for board certification by submitting 10 items (or "entries") documenting some aspect of their teaching performance. Four of these entries are contained in a portfolio that the candidate mails to the board in the spring. The portfolio, as described by NBPTS,[47] includes:

- One classroom-based entry with accompanying student work
- Two classroom-based entries that require video recordings of interactions between the teacher and students
- One documented accomplishments entry that provides evidence of the teacher's accomplishments outside of the classroom and how that work impacts student learning

Each entry, then, requires some direct evidence of teaching or school counseling as well as a commentary describing, analyzing, and reflecting on this evidence.

In addition to the portfolio, six exercises (comprised of an essay test of the teacher's knowledge of content and how to communicate it to students) are completed online. Entries are read by different teams of assessors, who score each entry on a 4-point scale. Some are double-rated for reliability purposes. Assessors can add or subtract 0.25 from each point on the scale, distinguishing, for example, a "3" from a "3 plus" (3.25) and a "3 minus" (2.75). The same scale is used to score the assessment center exercises. To receive a certificate, a candidate must obtain an average of 2.75 or better on the 10 entries. A weighted average is used, giving 60% weight to the four portfolio entries and 40% to assessment center exercises. Assessors' scores are averaged in order to determine the candidate's score on the item. Discrepancies between raters on the same entry of 1.5 or larger (on the 4-point scale) are resolved by one of the board's trainers.

The rubrics employed by the board state that a level-four entry must contain "clear, consistent, and convincing" evidence that standards are met; a level-3 entry need only contain "clear" evidence, a level-2 entry "limited" evidence, and a level-1 entry "little or no" evidence. As noted by Dale Ballou, since many assessor trainees do not find these distinctions sufficiently self-explanatory, the board also provides what it terms a "colloquial version" of its rubrics. A level-4 performance is to be considered "outrageously good," a level-3 "pretty darn good," a level-2 "mediocre, hints of accomplishment," and a level-1 "downright awful, weak." Dale Ballou finds fault with the whole process on five levels: a) lack of agreement on the criteria for assessing teacher performance, b) the slender evidentiary basis for assessment, c) the board's inability to authenticate or verify the accuracy of the materials it receives, d) the secrecy surrounding the board's assessments, and e) the involvement of teacher unions.[48]

As we saw in the previous chapter, many researchers have studied NBPTS certification and its connection to student outcomes. As we also saw, the results of these studies are mixed. It is possible, since participation in the program is voluntary, that NBPTS attracts already higher-performing teachers. As for the portfolio assessment process, no studies have examined the relationship between portfolio scores and student achievement. The studies that do exist have focused mainly on issues of validity and reliability, the use of NBTS in teacher training, or the effect of NBTS on teaching practice and contribution to teachers' greater understanding of their work.[49]

Summary

Portfolio assessment seems to be useful for assisting teachers, particularly those in training, to reflect on their work and to provide information about their practice across a broad spectrum of activities, many of which are not measurable from classroom observation. However, the very breadth of the data that may form portfolios makes it difficult to standardize their evaluation, and to achieve acceptable levels of inter-rater reliability. At the moment, portfolios may, at best, provide supplementary evidence of a teacher's best work for use in principal, mentor, or teacher trainer evaluations.

TEACHING ARTIFACTS

Another source of information for evaluating teachers (which may overlap slightly with teacher portfolios) is provided by the products or artifacts of their work, such as lesson plans, student work, assignments, and assessments. These artifacts of teaching may be subjected to an evaluation process that analyzes the potential contribution of artifacts to student learning by looking at variables such as their connection to standards, their depth, intellectual quality, and comprehensiveness. A few protocols for evaluating artifacts of teaching have been developed and used for research purposes.

Lindsay Clare and Pamela Aschbacher conducted an analysis of teacher assignments to see how well they were correlated with student work and evaluations from classroom observations.[50] They developed a rubric for evaluating assignments that consisted of scales measuring cognitive challenge, clarity of learning goals and grading criteria, alignment of goals with task and grading criteria, and overall quality. They found statistically significant correlations between the assignment ratings and two other indications of quality: student work (writing samples) and observed classroom practice (in English/language arts lessons). From this and other work by researchers at the National Center for Research on Evaluation, Standards and Student Testing (CRESST) at UCLA, the IQA was developed, which, as we saw in the previous chapter, includes student work samples and observations in addition to assignments, and showed some correlations with student achievement.

A research strand developed by Fred Newmann and his colleagues was designed to test the efficacy of a set of pedagogical standards that Newmann termed *authentic pedagogy*.[51] Authentic intellectual work for Newmann consists of three criteria: construction of knowledge, disciplined inquiry, and value beyond the school. The overall claim is that authentic intellectual work enables students to engage in higher-order thinking and real-world problem-solving rather than just routine use of facts and procedures. Where teachers aim for authentic student performance, they create assignments or assessment tasks that call upon students to construct their own meaning or knowledge, through in-depth disciplined inquiry. This in turn is linked to real-world problems that have meaning and applicability beyond success in school. Newmann and colleagues used a variety of methods for collecting information about teaching practice, including the collection of samples of assessment tasks. They found that students who received assignments that required more challenging intellectual work achieved greater than average gains on the Iowa Tests of Basic Skills in reading and mathematics, and demonstrated higher performance in reading, mathematics, and writing on the Illinois Goals Assessment Program. In addition, there was a strong relationship between the quality of teacher assignments and student work; that is, teachers who assigned more intellectually demanding tasks were more likely to get authentic intellectual work from students.

The aforementioned NBPTS portfolios contain classroom artifacts, which were the focus of study by Edward Silver and colleagues.[52] They concentrated on the mathematical features of the instructional tasks the teachers presented. They found that the teachers used a wide range of mathematics topics, but that these were not consistently intellectually challenging. They concluded that:

> even in lessons that teachers selected for display as best practice examples of teaching for understanding, innovative pedagogical approaches were not systematically used in ways that supported students' engagement with cognitively demanding mathematical tasks.[53]

Another tool called the Scoop Notebook for assessing classroom artifacts was developed by Hilda Borko and colleagues.[54] They had teachers "scoop" artifacts such as lesson plans, handouts, samples of student work, and grading rubrics into "packages" they called notebooks. Researchers then scored the notebooks on 11 dimensions and compared the resulting scores with ratings made by independent observers on the same dimensions. The independent raters' scores for the notebooks were similar to those from the independent observers. Borko and colleagues also found that the way in which science instruction was portrayed was similar across notebooks and observations. At the same time, they cautioned that artifact analyses may not yield reliable enough estimates of individual teachers' practice for use in judging that performance. In their study, agreement on exact ratings of notebook scores across dimensions was low (between 22% and 47%), and agreement within 1 point on a 5-point scale for the notebook rubrics was modest (between 75% and 91%). Furthermore, the researchers noted that inter-rater agreement was lower for notebooks in which teachers' reflections on their goals and context for the lessons submitted were limited, making some dimensions difficult for raters to judge. From two pilot studies, the authors assessed the reliability and validity of artifact collections as measures of math and science classroom practice. They concluded that, in general, researchers were able to rate classroom practice from an analysis of artifacts alone, "with a reasonable amount of agreement."[55] There were several problems and inconsistencies, however, indicating that an analysis of artifacts may have limited use for teacher evaluation if employed exclusively. Some other researchers have used the Scoop Notebook in combination with other measures to evaluate science or math teaching.[56]

Summary

Collected classroom artifacts may provide information about a teacher's practice that is more easily obtained than through classroom observation, and more reliable than self-report data from teachers. However, there remain questions about reliability in the scoring of these artifacts, as well as complications related to the extensive training necessary for raters that make this option unrealistic for most non-research settings and for accountability purposes. No studies have been conducted to relate artifact assessment and student achievement. Artifact assessment may, however, provide a useful method for measuring classroom practice.

TEACHER SELF-REPORTS

An economical method for assessing classroom practice is to collect reports from teachers, either by interview, questionnaire, or teacher logs and diaries. An obvious concern with asking teachers about their practice is the danger that they will provide biased responses that paint an inflated picture about what they do in the classroom. Some studies have addressed this validity question by comparing teacher reports with other measures, such as artifacts or classroom observations, and some have compared logs with teacher surveys.

Leigh Burstein and colleagues from RAND Corporation were contracted by the National Science Foundation (NSF) in the mid-1990s to examine instructional practices using classroom artifacts, teacher surveys, and teacher logs.[57] Burstein and colleagues designed their study to investigate the instructional content, goals, and strategies used in secondary mathematics classrooms. The study included 70 mathematics teachers from nine schools in two states. Over 5 weeks, the researchers collected assignments and exams and the teachers completed daily logs in which they reported what they taught and how they taught it. Teachers also completed two surveys, one given at the beginning of the study period, prior to the collection of the artifact data, and the other at the end of the semester. The surveys asked teachers to describe the instructional practices they used (or were going to use) and the topics they covered (or were planning to cover). The researchers also reviewed the course textbooks and considered both the reliability and the validity of the surveys and logs, the two kinds of teacher report data.

They found that, for 9 of the 13 items of classroom practice, the agreement between the end-of-semester surveys and logs was below 51% and for all items under 60%. This was considered a quite low rate of agreement by the authors. The resulting lack of overlap between logs and surveys does not allow a conclusion that the surveys are reliable. At the same time, because we cannot explain the statistical disagreement, we also cannot conclude that they are unreliable. Since both the logs and the surveys are subjective data, they cannot be used together to check validity. The classroom artifacts have the potential to serve as a validity check, and the authors did make this comparison, but with only limited success. They found that classroom artifacts were not useful as a means of validating instructional practice, partly because they were unable to assess from artifacts such as textbooks and assignments the amount of class time that was spent in given activities. They *were* able to conclude, however, that within their limited ability to validate the survey data (for example, on items such as exams and homework assignments), they found the data to represent accurately the instructional strategies used by the teachers.

The Study of Instructional Improvement (SII) was a longitudinal study of literacy instruction in schools that were implementing three comprehensive school reforms: the Accelerated Schools Project, America's Choice, and Success for All. It was conducted in the period 2000–2004 by a collaborative group of researchers who worked mainly through the Consortium for Policy Research in Education whose home base is the University of Pennsylvania.[58] This group used more than 75,000 teacher logs from almost 2,000 1st- to 5th-grade teachers. They chose logs as a good middle ground between classroom observation (which is the "gold standard" but expensive) and teacher surveys (which are of questionable accuracy and validity).[59] One study, for example, compared data from logs and teacher surveys and found that teachers uniformly reported higher frequencies for using teaching practices on the annual questionnaires than they did on the log.[60] Another study showed high responses rates for logs (90% of teachers completed them) and demonstrated that the data collected through logs were only slightly less accurate than those collected by trained observers.[61] Although log data may be cheaper to collect than observational data (but more expensive than surveys), SII researchers found their analysis to be challenging.[62] After reviewing all the studies connected with the project, SII researchers concluded that, for most study purposes, collection of about 20 logs (evenly spaced over the academic year) "should allow researchers to reliably discriminate instructional practices in the area of reading/language arts across teachers and schools."[63] They found logs to have strong construct validity and to constitute a viable method of data collection in large-sample research on teaching.

Daniel Mayer from Mathematica Policy Research questioned whether survey data could be trusted to provide accurate information about instructional practice.[64] He observed algebra teachers and recorded the amount of time they spent in practices that were consistent with the professional standards for math teaching set by the National Council of Teachers of Mathematics (NCTM).[65] He also used a 34-item survey to discover from teachers how much time over the year they reported using 17 different practices related to the standards. Mayer found that the observed and reported measures were highly correlated, but the teachers' responses were systematically inflated. Further, the estimates of individual practices were unreliable. While the composite measures of practice were valid regarding the amount of time the practices were used, they provided no information about the quality of the instruction. Mayer concluded that more information was needed about both the validity and reliability of these measures.

Some researchers choose to collect information about classroom practice by interviewing teachers, mostly as a qualitative supplement to quantitative data. Usually situationally specific, interviews are unlikely to be accompanied by information about their reliability and validity.

Summary

Teacher self-reported data, whether through surveys, logs, or interviews, provide insights about practice that may be obtained at lower cost than through direct observation. Some evidence suggests that logs provide data that are almost as reliable as the data collected by trained observers, but researchers must always be wary of human beings' tendency to present themselves as favorably as possible. Self-report data have the advantage of being able to address teachers' intentions as well as their knowledge and beliefs about teaching. Of particular value in mentoring or professional development settings, self-report data may play a more important role for formative than for summative purposes.

STUDENT RATINGS

Although students have the most intimate and consistent knowledge about what their teachers do in the classroom, theirs are the opinions least frequently sought for the purposes of teacher evaluation. Student evaluations are most often used in higher education settings where there are numerous reasons for considering them valid.[66] For example, students are good, if not the best, judges of their own changes in knowledge or motivation; of teacher characteristics such as punctuality, legibility of writing, and enthusiasm; and of aspects of practice such as questioning habits and frequency of tests or quizzes. Children may be less dependable than college students as sources of information about their teachers, however. Nevertheless, the researchers involved in the Gates Foundation MET Project (under the leadership of Tom Kane) are including student evaluations in their effort to find reliable measures of effective teaching at the K–12 level.

The most recent reviews of studies that examined K–12 student ratings of teacher effectiveness were conducted by John Follman in the 1990s.[67] Although not a common focus of research today, secondary students' ratings of teachers were studied frequently up until the latter decades of the last century. Elementary student ratings were less often considered. Follman concluded from his review of the literature on pupil ratings of teachers that, although there are certain aspects of teaching such as teacher's content knowledge or choice of pedagogy that students are not qualified to judge, student ratings of certain events occurring in the class as well as teacher interactions can be objective, reliable, and valid. He recognizes that younger students are vulnerable to rating leniency and halo effects, but goes so far as to recommend that student ratings should be included as part of teacher evaluations, even for high-stakes purposes such as merit pay and career ladder decisions.

VALUE-ADDED MODELING (VAM)

Measuring student growth through value-added modeling (VAM) is now a widely used method for assessing school and teacher effectiveness. As more and more school districts compile their databases of student test scores so that teachers and students can be linked across the years, the option for calculating value-added scores becomes more broadly available. Tennessee was the first state to institute a value-added system, largely influenced by the work of William Sanders and his colleagues, who demonstrated the lasting effects of having a good teacher, and that teachers are the single most important contributor to student achievement.[68] Districts in other states such as Texas and Ohio have followed suit. However, VAM is dogged by considerable controversy. This was brought to a head when the *Los Angeles Times* accessed the 7-year test-score database of the Los Angeles Unified

School District, had a statistician from the RAND Corporation calculate value-added scores for each teacher, and then made the teacher rankings available to any member of the public who was interested in finding them out.[69]

VAM is controversial on two main counts: how it is calculated and how it is used. We will examine both of these questions briefly. For a more thorough exposition of the issues, the reader is directed to one of several recent publications.[70] There is no argument that VAM is superior to other available models. The report from a 2008 workshop on VAM describes four kinds of test-based evaluation models: status models, cohort-to-cohort change models, growth models, and value-added models.[71] They are distinguished by the kinds of policy-related questions they are able to address. Status models describe student performance at a given time and are useful for identifying the percentage of students who are performing at a desired level. Cohort-to-cohort change models compare status at two points in time, but for different sets of students. Thus, a school district might compare the math performance of this year's 6th-graders with that of last year's 6th-graders. Growth models compare the same students across years to establish how much they have gained between, say, the 5th- and 6th-grade school years. They measure growth, but do not say anything about what might have been the cause of that growth. Value-added models are growth models that use statistical methods to control for school and student background factors in order to be able to attribute changes in student performance to the school or teacher or program.

How Value-Added Scores Are Calculated

Like any statistical model, VAMs can be written as an equation in which some measure of achievement (represented in the left-hand side of the equation) is expressed as a function of any number of explanatory variables (represented in the right hand side of the equation). The first set of challenges against value-added models concerns the left side of the equation—namely, the exclusive focus on standardized test scores. Standardized tests tap only a narrow area of knowledge and skills. Not all subjects are tested and not all aspects of knowledge are quizzed in the subjects that are tested. Further, other goals of schooling such as the development of intellectual curiosity, civic mindedness, and motivation for learning are outside the reach of standardized tests. Tests are not equivalent from one grade level to the next in the way that two versions of the same test might be, yielding so-called linkages between grade levels that are weaker than one would like. Attempts to vertically link tests across grade levels may lead to emphasis on certain kinds of knowledge that easily span grades and an avoidance of subject elements that may be just as important but not common to both grade levels. This may have the effect of either causing teachers to focus on some domains of the subject matter and not others, or making teachers appear less effective if their students are not tested on material that they have learned well. Dale Ballou has raised an additional question about the scaling of questions in the standardized tests upon which VAM is based. He suggests that instead of assuming an interval scale (where a 5-point difference from 55 to 60 is considered the same as a 5-point difference from 85 to 90), value-added models should consider using an ordinal analysis, so changing the question that would be asked. Thus, we would be inquiring what fraction of the target teacher's students outperforms the students of the (hypothetical) average instructor, rather than looking at the mean achievement of a teacher's students against those of the average instructor.[72] In the face of these concerns, it is often reasonably argued that multiple measures of learning should be used to estimate school, program, or teacher effectiveness because test scores are too narrow a representation of what a student knows or should know, and are open to problems of vertical linkage and item scaling.

Even if one accepts that gains in standardized test scores present a useful picture of the quality of a school, program, or teacher, gains need to be calculated with a minimum of error and a careful selection of variables that belong on the right-hand side of the equation because they might contribute to student learning. Controls for other variables are needed because students are usually not randomly assigned to teachers. Possible influences on test scores include other teaching sources such as tutors, parents, previous teachers, the Internet, or summer school, which in turn may be influenced by parental income, which may relate to school attendance and student health. School factors such as curriculum materials, technology access, class size, pull-out programs, and second language support may also affect learning. Some value-added models attempt to control for certain of these factors, particularly poverty levels, race, and English language status, but there are limits to the statistical possibilities for controlling for all possible relevant variables effectively.

In summary, there are at least four distinct issues that face the statistician attempting to construct the right-hand side of the VAM equation in an attempt to estimate the value that a teacher has added to her students' learning over the year. First is whether and/or how to control for student background. William Sanders argues that his model, developed originally for use in Tennessee (known as TVAAS, the Tennessee Value Added Assessment System[73]), implicitly controls for socioeconomic status and background variables because each student acts effectively as his own control.[74] Other educational researchers and statisticians have taken issue with this position, arguing forcefully that student demographic variables should be included in the model.[75] This is the accepted practice in the United Kingdom, where educators now refer to "contextual" value-added (CVA) models to distinguish them from the earlier versions that used prior attainment only.[76] The Sanders group's response is that attempts to correct for the socio-economic correlations by including demographic variables in the analysis "may actually exacerbate the bias in the educational effects."[77] They suggest that the best protection against incorrectly rating a teacher is to use multiple pre-test scores, especially for the scenario where the least capable teachers are assigned to the highest-poverty classrooms.

The second issue concerns the confusion of school effects with teacher effects. One solution for avoiding such confusion is to construct a school fixed-effects model that includes predictor variables for each school.[78] However, by eliminating school differences from average teacher quality, any comparison of teachers among schools in this model assumes (incorrectly) that all schools hire teachers of equal skill.[79]

A third challenge for VAM is whether teacher effects remain stable across time. In general, estimates appear at best moderately stable within teachers across time, with some researchers finding relatively unstable year-to-year correlations.[80] One study of mathematics teachers in Florida found moderate correlations (of about 0.3) between estimated effects for the same teacher across adjacent school years, a relationship that the authors felt, given the large sampling errors, represented fairly stable effects for teachers across time, but are certainly not overwhelming.[81] Similar results were found in a large urban school district in Tennessee.[82] Perhaps the most comprehensive study of inter-temporal stability so far has been conducted by Dan Goldhaber and Michael Hansen.[83] They examined an 11-year panel of data from North Carolina schools with the goal of considering the use of VAM for making decisions about teacher tenure. Their unique database allowed them to investigate the changes in the stability of teacher estimates over a longer time frame than had been used in previous studies, assess the stability of multiple-year estimates of teacher effects, and examine the degree to which early career estimates of teacher effects predict the achievement of students taught later in a teacher's career, specifically pre- and post-tenure. Their careful analysis takes into account many factors such as different value-added models, teacher years of experience (that may reflect changes in ability and/or narrowing of job performance as more productive teachers are promoted out of the classroom and less productive teachers are counseled out of the profession), convergence to school norms, and certain school conditions (such as whether the principal is new). They found that estimated prior performance is a good predictor of estimated future performance of teachers. They consider this an important finding for certain policy decisions, but indicate that tenure-related decisions likely would require a higher standard, since there would be a lag between the time that VAMs could be estimated and tenure decisions were made. Their findings certainly imply that VAM teacher effect estimates serve as better indicators of teacher quality than observable teacher attributes, even when a 3-year lag between the time that the estimates are derived and student achievement is predicted. They postulate that to remove the lowest 25% of teachers would have "an educationally significant effect" on the distribution of teacher quality of the remaining teachers.[84]

The fourth question relates to teacher effects across different kinds of students. Although there is plenty of anecdotal evidence to suggest that some teachers are more effective with certain kinds of students than with others (and this is often the source of non-random assignments of students to teachers by principals), there is little definitive research on this issue, although we have seen that some researchers have found a connection between the race or gender of teacher and students.[85] If there is a possibility for teachers to be differentially effective with different students (say, with high achievers or with those who are struggling), then it should be a consideration in the construction of value-added estimates.[86]

How Value-Added Scores Are Used

As data become more accessible and VAM increases in sophistication, some institutions, including the U.S. government, are pushing to use student achievement data for accountability purposes. A widely distributed report from the New Teacher Project entitled *The Widget Effect* [87] demonstrates how rarely school districts either deal with incompetence or reward excellence.[88] The authors recommend the adoption of a performance evaluation system that differentiates teachers according to their effectiveness in promoting student achievement. Michelle Rhee took this recommendation to heart in the D.C. schools, where she abandoned teacher tenure, implemented a new comprehensive evaluation system that combined value-added scores with classroom observations, and fired several hundred teachers in her first year as head of the school system. While applauding the move from highly subjective evaluations to ratings based on empirical data, many statisticians, economists, and educational researchers are exhorting school administrators to exercise caution in using value-added scores for high-stakes decisions, even though VAM is widely recognized as providing the most powerful computation of school, program, or teacher effectiveness.[89] Public discussions multiplied after the *L.A. Times* published its series of articles on teacher effectiveness in the L.A. Unified Schools. The publication of teachers' names and their effectiveness rankings raised issues of journalistic ethics and public policy in addition to the questions about the reliability of VAM and the achievement tests upon which they are based.[90] In defense of VAM, William Sanders, who was the first to apply this technique to education, maintains:

> if you use rigorous, robust methods and surround them with safeguards, you can reliably distinguish highly effective teachers from average teachers and from ineffective teachers.[91]

However, even Sanders does not advocate the use of VAM for making decisions about individual teachers.[92]

Summary

Increased focus on accountability, teacher effectiveness, teacher quality, merit pay, and standardized test scores has resulted in efforts to measure the relationship between what teachers do and how much students learn. VAM is one method for estimating the effects of schools, teachers, or programs on changes in students' test scores. As statisticians, economists, and educational researchers devote their attention to improving VAM methodology, we get closer to linking teacher inputs with student outputs. However, we are still far from being able to estimate a teacher's effectiveness solely from test scores, and even if we could, value-added scores will never be any better than the tests from which they are derived—not that I think anyone has gone on record advocating that VAM should be used as the only source of information for making high-stakes decisions about teachers and schools. There does appear to be a consensus that value-added scores should constitute one component for evaluating teachers, under certain conditions, and with certain caveats. The long list of criticisms of standardized tests, and of the potential pitfalls in the construction of value-added models, is, in itself, not sufficient for us to dismiss VAM out of hand. Some of the problems are more serious than others and some can be solved by appropriate statistical modeling. Even with its guaranteed imperfection, VAM is a better indicator of effectiveness than the alternatives. At present, promotion and other high-stakes decisions are based on a combination of observational evaluation by administrators, years of experience, and advanced degrees. As we have seen, experience only makes a difference early in a teacher's career, and advanced degrees appear to have no bearing on teacher quality. Administrator ratings tend to be inflated, and it is not clear whether principals are capable of identifying effective teachers when they observe them. We shall see from my own experiments described in the next chapter that principals are not able to distinguish between effective and ineffective teachers as measured by histories of low or high student growth.

MEASURING TEACHER QUALITY—ASSESSING THE EVIDENCE

The more effort that researchers devote to devising efficient measures of teaching practice and accurate calculations of student achievement, the closer we will get to understanding the causal relationship between the two. Several protocols exist that produce an extensive evaluation of teaching practice from classroom observations, some focusing on specific subjects and others on certain grade levels, and some that attempt to span both subject and level. For the most part, these observation protocols are more useful for researchers than for administrators who need to produce evaluations for accountability purposes and are unlikely to take the necessary time for training and multiple visits to the classroom. Further, in general, research on the relation between classroom observations of teaching and student test scores shows at best a mild correlation that is not strong enough for making high-stakes decisions. Most principal evaluations appear to be pro forma, however, with very few teachers receiving a less-than-satisfactory rating. Some studies of teacher evaluations by principals in a research setting suggest that school administrators have some success at identifying successful teachers. Since principals have information about the teachers from other sources, such as parent input, previous test scores, and reports from previous principals, these studies are not a true test of a principal's ability to identify teacher effectiveness exclusively from classroom observations. Disagreements about how best to construct value-added models and the fact that they rely solely on standardized tests limit VAM's potential for providing the sole measure of school, program, or teacher effectiveness. The most conservative approach, and the one that is advocated most often, is to combine information obtained from VAMs with some other measure, such as observation, portfolios, or student evaluations, in order to arrive at an estimate of teacher effectiveness that can then be used to make decisions about promotion, merit pay, or firing.

5

Experiments in the Identification of Successful Teachers

We have seen that classroom observation instruments tend to be normatively rather than empirically based. That is, most are constructed with items that rate teaching practice against a set of state or national standards rather than against elements of practice that have shown empirical connections to student outcomes. We have also seen that researchers have studied some of the more widely used instruments, such as the Danielson Framework and Pianta et al.'s CLASS, to determine how well scores on these instruments predict student achievement. They don't come off too well, at least not with enough strength to form the basis for making any high-stakes decisions. We have also seen that most of the time when school administrators evaluate teachers they give them at least a satisfactory rating, even though we know that 97% of the teachers in America are not performing at satisfactory levels. Under experimental conditions, administrator ratings reflect a greater range, and even though there are a couple of studies that indicate their evaluations are correlated with student achievement, it is not clear to what extent the evaluation relies on information outside of that gained from classroom observation, such as previous test scores, recommendations from other principals, peer reviews, and so on.

Given this picture presented by the existing research, I was prompted to consider two questions. First, if educators and others are presented with opportunities to observe teachers with established records of raising or lowering student achievement, how successful would they be in correctly identifying the more and less effective teachers? Second, is it desirable and possible to develop an observation measure that has higher levels of predictability with regard to a teacher's ability to raise student achievement scores that currently exists?

My experience talking to school administrators is that they think they are good at identifying effective teachers when they see them. This fact was confirmed by at least one school superintendent who was interviewed by Robert Siegel of National Public Radio in a segment of the show *All Things Considered* where they were discussing the use of value-added scores in the aftermath of the *LA Times* story mentioned earlier. Here is an excerpt of the show's transcript:

> *Siegel*: And how big a part does value-added analysis play in your assessment of your teachers?
>
> *Dr. Martin*: Well, it's certainly an important part for teachers. It's also an important part for schools. I will say that our state board of education, I think very wisely, passed a policy that says that information is exactly like the teacher evaluation instrument that we would have in a person's, you know, permanent record file.
>
> *Siegel*: And therefore, it's not public information?
>
> *Dr. Martin*: It is not public information in North Carolina. It is treated as your evaluation document, and it is confidential information.
>
> *Siegel*: But how big a factor of a teacher's evaluation is it, that analysis?
>
> *Dr. Martin*: Well, for us, if you have—the system is very simple. It's red, yellow and green. Those are pretty easy ways to look at it. And if you're red, your students are performing two standard errors below your—sort of comparable counterparts. If you're yellow, you're right in the average performance. And if you're green, you're two standard errors above.
>
> And if a teacher has one red, you know, their first year, then we literally just have a—it's like a growth conference with them. They have a personal, you know, individual plan. We talk to them about what are they going to do differently next year.
>
> Then in the second year, if there's two reds in a row, the teacher has consecutive reds, then we have a trigger for what we call a plan of assistance. And that plan of assistance may involve going to training. It may involve sending in some central office folks to work with that person and to really work on, you know, a very formal plan that's now, you know—could trigger dismissal at the end of the year if it is unsuccessful.
>
> *Siegel*: Let me ask you this question about value-added analysis. If I said, here are 10 classrooms. And five of them are teachers who have red ratings, and five of them have greens. And I didn't tell you who is who and you went and looked at the classrooms, do you think you would be able to figure out who the greens are, and who were the reds are? Or is this information at odds or irrelevant to standard ways of evaluating teachers' performance in the classroom?
>
> *Dr. Martin*: In a single observation—I actually think you might be able to in a single observation. I'm sure you could in multiple operations—multiple observations.
>
> *Siegel*: And principals typically are not surprised to learn who's the red and who's the green? Those are the teachers they assume would be in those categories?

Dr. Martin: They are not surprised. I think if you—across the country, though, you will find that teacher-evaluation systems are, you know, kind of a Lake Wobegon issue. Everybody is above average.

Siegel: Hm-mm.

Dr. Martin: And I think you will find that. There's always the wiggle room and the culture. And it's not just a school district culture. It's almost a national culture of teacher evaluations. And I look at that if there's somebody to blame, its central office, it's our group that's to blame. And we have to talk about—sort of an honesty in the evaluation process.

Siegel: Well, what do you make of the *L.A. Times* decision to make the information public?

Dr. Martin: Well . . .

Siegel: If it's very useful, why shouldn't parents know this—who's doing well?

Dr. Martin: Well, it's the kind—you know, if we had 10 people for every job, and you could just dismiss every one and do that cause if you get—it's just like with any evaluation instrument. We have a duty and in fact, we have to by necessity, you know, try to work with our teachers and improve their instruction. We've got to work with them to perform.

Siegel: But just to summarize, as for what the *L.A. Times* did, if that were done in your system, you would not welcome that—is what I hear you say?

Dr. Martin: Exactly. I would not welcome that because I think—and I'm glad it's basically against our state board policy.

Siegel: Yeah.

Dr. Martin: I mean, I think that's good.

Siegel: Superintendent Martin, thank you very much for talking with us.

Dr. Martin: Thank you.

Siegel: That's Donald Martin, who is superintendent in the North Carolina Winston-Salem/Forsyth County School District.

Dr. Martin is not alone in thinking he is able to identify a "red" from a "green" teacher on a single visit to the classroom. Principals and other school administrators often report to me that their years of experience enable them to identify the quality of a teacher within minutes of entering their classrooms. To bring this question out of the realm of anecdote and to address it scientifically, I developed a set of experiments involving teachers for whom I had historical value-added data, and whom I was able to film during regular classroom lessons. I will shortly describe these experiments and what we found.[1]

Before we get to the experiments, however, I want to provide some background research from the fields of psychology and cognitive science that examines what goes on in people's minds as they make judgments about human behavior. It is startling to me that rarely in the educational research literature on classroom observation is there any reference to or acknowledgment of the cognitive processes involved in making judgments of human behavior. I described these processes in detail in an earlier book,[2] and so a summary will suffice here.

COGNITIVE OPERATIONS

One possible contributing explanation for the weak correlations between existing teacher observation instruments and teacher effectiveness as measured by student achievement is that judgments made during classroom observations may be influenced, and therefore biased, by various cognitive operations. Cognitive psychologists have identified a variety of phenomena that influence how our mind works when we observe and make judgments. For example, *confirmation bias* describes a tendency to seek, embellish, and emphasize experiences that support rather than challenge already held beliefs.[3] Thus, if we have some preconceptions about a teacher we are going to observe, these might influence what we see, regardless of the behavior we actually witness when we visit the classroom. *Motivated reasoning*, the converse of confirmation bias, suggests that we look more skeptically at data that do not fit our beliefs than those that do.[4] Thus, if we believe in the superiority of a certain method for teaching science and we see a teacher using a different method, even though the children appear to be engrossed in the work and learning successfully, we may look for reasons to criticize the lesson. *Inattentional blindness*[5] is a striking occurrence in which people fail to notice stimuli appearing in front of their eyes when they are preoccupied with a task that demands full attention. This is demonstrated in an experiment where observers fail to notice a gorilla walking in front of a group of basketball players, when they are focused on counting how many times a basketball is passed. In a classroom observation setting, we may be trying to focus on one aspect of classroom dynamics, such as how often the teacher calls on boys rather than girls, or which children raise their hands when the teacher asks a question, and in so doing, we fail to notice other important events such as one student tutoring another, or a student vigorously texting rather than working on the assigned project.

Channel capacity[6] is a concept from the literature on information processing that refers to the fact that there is an upper limit of an observer's ability to match his or her responses to a given set of stimuli. It comes into play immediately for an observer who is required to rate a teacher on 60+ items over a 20-minute period (which is characteristic of many of the instruments in use). Typical strategies for dealing with the limits of channel capacity are to chunk information, omit information, or generalize across items. Herbert Simon's concept of *bounded rationality* describes the simplified model of reality that we construct because the mind cannot cope directly with the complexity of the world (or the classroom).

Further study by psychologists in the field of perception has exposed a variety of phenomena that induce errors in how we process what we experience through the senses. These include the idea that we are influenced by our expectations and preconceptions. In other words, we see what we expect to see (and hear what we expect to hear). Also, perception is influenced by context and by perspective. The same classroom events may receive different interpretations from students, teachers, or principals. Psychologists have also demonstrated that we are quick to form initial impressions and slow to change them, even if they were derived from incomplete or ambiguous information. This is known as *belief perseverance,*[7] and has been demonstrated in several experiments, many of them from the fields of business and economics.[8] Once we are confronted with the evidence that discounts our original perceptions, however, we tend to rationalize after the fact, a phenomenon known as *hindsight bias.*[9] This describes the tendency to see events that have occurred as more predictable than they had been before they took place. In a school setting, it may come into play when a principal looks back on a classroom evaluation after subsequently looking at some test-score data, or receiving a report from a parent.

In summary, this research provides the following alerts for anyone looking to conduct classroom observations:

- We tend to seek out confirmation of existing beliefs.
- We tend to dismiss what we do not expect to see.
- If we are focusing on one thing, we tend to miss other things.
- We can focus on only so many things at once.
- We tend to see what we expect to see.
- What we see is influenced by perspective and context.
- We tend to form judgments quickly, and they are highly resistant to change.
- When we do change a judgment, we look back at the original evidence as if it had been more predictive than it was.

One useful way of conceptualizing these various cognitive operations is to frame them around two generic modes of cognitive function that describe what we might think of as *intuitive* versus *deliberate* or *rational* thought processes. Philosophers, dating back to Socrates, and psychologists over the past century have conceptualized them in this manner.[10] More recently, researchers have further emphasized and defined the distinction between these dual systems of cognitive processes: those executed quickly with little conscious deliberation and those that are slower and more reflective.[11] Keith Stanovich and Richard West called these "System 1" and "System 2" processes.[12] The operations of System 1 are fast, automatic, effortless, associative, and difficult to control or modify, whereas those of System 2 are slower, serial, effortful, and deliberately controlled; they are also relatively flexible and potentially rule-governed.

System 1 operations produce shortcuts, or heuristics, that allow us to function rapidly and effectively. A program of research studies (known now as the heuristics and biases approach) conducted by Daniel Kahneman and colleagues has documented the persistence of systematic errors in the intuitions of experts, implying that their intuitive judgments may be endorsed, at least passively, by their rational processes from System 2, one of whose functions is to monitor the quality both of mental operations and overt behavior.[13] These studies suggest that the monitoring is normally quite lax, and allows many erroneous intuitive judgments to be expressed, along with the correct ones. Shane Frederick demonstrated this clearly in an experiment where he found that quite large percentages of highly intelligent college students failed to reject plausible but erroneous solutions to simple puzzles.[14] The surprisingly high rate of errors in these easy problems illustrates how lightly the output of System 1 is monitored by System 2.

System 2 judgments are less often erroneous than System 1 judgments, and since the path to the result is conscious, errors can be corrected. Much of the unreliability in human judgment comes from our inability or disinclination to use System 2. This work is nicely described and summarized in Kahneman's lecture when he won the Nobel Prize for economics in 2002.[15] Thus, in a classroom setting, we can imagine that an observer will generate both System 1 and System 2 judgments. However, we do not know how systematic and widespread the influence of operations from System 1 is, but we may hypothesize that these operations could contribute to the apparent lack of success in predicting learning outcomes from observations of teaching behavior.

THE EXPERIMENTS

In order to test whether observers can accurately distinguish between effective and ineffective teachers and to discover what criteria they use in making judgments, I designed a set of experiments whereby a variety of judges were given the opportunity to rate teachers of known levels of effectiveness. In order to be able to present a number of samples of teaching to judges under experimental conditions, we used a technique known as "thin slicing" that has been used by researchers from a number of different fields. Thin slicing derives from the consistent finding that judgments about other people made from short samples of their behavior, sometimes as fleeting as a few seconds, tend to be highly predictive of judgments based on much longer samples. A thin slice is defined as a brief (i.e., shorter than 5 minutes) excerpt of expressive behavior sampled from the behavioral stream.[16] Previous work has demonstrated that thin slices can provide information about a range of psychological constructs, including dispositional characteristics, social relations, and job performance.[17] This technique has been used in a variety of settings, including education, where researchers found that students could predict a professor's end-of-semester class evaluations from exposure to a few seconds of their filmed lecturing.[18] More recently, thin slicing has been used to test naïve subjects' ability to forecast the outcomes of gubernatorial elections by viewing short clips of their debates, finding them to be more accurate in their predictions than models based on economic circumstances.[19] This body of research demonstrates that it is possible to obtain dependable ratings from a large number of participants without requiring lengthy laboratory sessions. For my purposes, it meant that we could show observers short segments from filmed lessons and still be confident that the resulting judgments would be highly indicative of those based on viewing films of longer excerpts or even the whole lessons. Consequently, the penalty that we should expect to pay for using thin slices, if any, is in terms of the precision of judgments, not their overall accuracy. It is important to note that thin slicing is not far removed from what often occurs and what is sometimes advocated in the real world when school principals evaluate teachers. See, for example, *The Three-Minute Classroom Walkthrough*.[20] However, the appropriateness of thin slicing for the experiment is not intended to suggest an endorsement of short walkthroughs as a viable or reliable method for administrators to evaluate teachers.

Experiment 1

The first step was to review data from a school district whereby we could calculate value-added scores for the teachers over a number of years in the manner of the *LA Times* procedure.[21] We focused on math scores at the elementary level since previous research suggested there was a greater connection between observation and achievement in math than in language arts, and students get input from only one teacher in the elementary grades. We then identified teachers in the database whose value-added scores indicated that their effectiveness was consistently higher or lower than average over the prior 3 years. This resulted in two groups with a difference in mean value-added scores of roughly a 0.50 standard deviations. We randomly selected teachers from the high and low effectiveness groups, obtained their approval to participate, and filmed them during a regular lesson. We showed short excerpts of these films to judges from various backgrounds and asked them to decide to which group each teacher belonged and to explain the rationale for their choices.

The teachers whom we filmed all worked in a medium-sized Californian school district that conducted annual testing and maintained a database of student test scores linked to teachers by unique identifiers, thereby enabling us to estimate value-added scores. Fourth-grade teachers who had a 3-year history of classes that performed at least one-half a standard deviation above the mean in math value-added gains constituted the high group. The low group consisted of 4th-grade teachers whose classes had not achieved gains of at least one-half a standard deviation above the mean in any of the previous 3 years. This identification produced a possible pool of almost 30 teachers, 10 of whom were randomly selected for participation, allowing for some with higher and some with lower performance records. If a teacher declined the offer, he or she was replaced with a randomly drawn substitute.

Researchers contacted the teachers and offered them $100 as compensation for permitting us to film a lesson on fractions. Ten White, female teachers formed the final sample of those who agreed to be filmed. One subsequently withdrew her consent, and two films were of poor quality, leaving us with seven teachers in the sample, three from the high and four from the low group, who were separated by 0.50 standard deviations or more in the VAM scores. The seven teachers had between 7 and 19 years of classroom experience. Age and experience were equally distributed across high and low groups. All had elementary teaching credentials and none was a math specialist.

A total of 100 judges took part in Experiment 1. These were distributed among 10 categories: school administrators, education professors, math educators, teacher educators, parents of elementary schoolchildren, K–12 teachers, undergraduate students taking education courses, teacher mentors, elementary schoolchildren, and adults with no formal connection to education. The purpose of selecting judges from different backgrounds was to determine whether their relationship to education affected their judgments. Judges were recruited through various means, including personal invitation, flyers distributed in educational establishments, and word-of-mouth. Recruitment continued until we had administered 100 sessions distributed across the 10 categories of judge.

We extracted 2-minute segments from each of the seven films using a commercial computer digital editing program. At this point, all researchers except the statistician who calculated the value-added scores were still blind to the group affiliation of the teachers. Each clip featured the teacher presenting part of a lesson on fractions to the whole class. In most cases, we selected the first two consecutive minutes of *whole-class instruction* that occurred in the lesson.[22] Exceptions were made if an interruption occurred, such as the phone ringing or a behavior management episode, in which case the next 2 consecutive minutes were chosen. In all cases, these clips occurred no sooner than 11 minutes into the 50-minute lesson and no later than 19 minutes before the end of the lesson. Clips were labeled with a teacher number. We constructed 10 playlists using different random orders of the seven clips. We designed score sheets listing each teacher by number with a small still photo and an option for the observer to check "yes" if that teacher were judged to be in the high group or "no" for the low group. A debriefing interview questioned the judges about their educational background and experience, the criteria they used to make their selections, their confidence in their judgments, and their perceptions about the task itself.

A researcher, blind to the group affiliation of the teachers, administered the experiment individually with each of the 100 participants in any available quiet setting, usually a private office. Each participant then viewed a randomly selected playlist of the seven clips on a notebook computer using a headset. Each clip was separated by a 30-second pause for completing the score sheet, where they recorded whether or not the teacher was in the above-average group, and any notes they wished to help them in their judgments. They were told that the clips had been randomly chosen from a larger sample and that any clip could be of a teacher in either group. After the participant had viewed all seven clips and completed the score sheet, the researcher conducted the debriefing interview, lasting about 15 minutes. This interview was audio-recorded.

We were interested primarily in the extent to which judges agreed with one another in their choices and how accurately they could place the teachers in their respective groups. Also of interest were the factors on which they based their judgments. So what did we find? Well, first of all, with regard to agreement, individually, inter-judge correlations were quite low (0.24) but aggregated across judges the correlation was a high 0.97, indicating a sound basis for estimating a global relationship between VAM scores and the judgments of observers as a group. As far as accuracy was concerned, the level (2.8 out of a possible 7) was slightly below what would have been expected by chance (3.5). Further statistical analysis suggested that an effective strategy for identifying teachers accurately would be to place them in the *opposite* categories to which the judges assigned them, resulting in correct classifications almost two-thirds of the time! We also looked at whether judges were equally accurate (or inaccurate) when judging each teacher. Again, a simple count brought this into doubt. Three of the teachers (one high and two low) were accurately rated by between 62% and 69% of the judges, while four were accurately rated by only 15–30% of the judges. Curiously, the highest agreements were for teachers who were inaccurately assigned to the high or low group. There appeared to be no benefit from expertise in education, since the elementary schoolchildren had the best accuracy record (about equal to chance). Whatever was driving the systematic nature of the judgments and their inaccuracy, it was something to which educational experts were not immune.

The factors influencing subjects' judgments fell into four distinct categories: student engagement, teaching strategies, teacher characteristics, and math knowledge. The most frequently cited indicator was the level of student engagement. Eleven different teaching strategies were mentioned with some frequency in the debriefing sessions, with the most common being "accessing students' prior knowledge," "having active interaction with the students," and "moving around the classroom." The subjects referred to two kinds of teacher characteristics. Forty-five percent mentioned the teachers' confidence, energy, or "presence," and 10% valued a teacher with a sense of humor or an engaging personality.

The impressive rate of agreement among judges overall suggests that, regardless of background, judges were responding to systematic influences. At the same time, the judgments made by both expert and non-expert judges were inaccurate in ways that also reflected systematic influences—certain teachers were inaccurately rated by a significant majority of judges while others were not, and the accuracy of judges overall was significantly lower than would have been produced by chance. Given this, it appears that non-random influences, possibly System 1 operations, appear to have led judges astray. Here are the most likely explanations for the findings.

1. *Biased VAM scores:* There is reason to believe that VAM scores estimated with linear regression, like the ones we used, can be biased.[23] This might cause accurate judges to appear erroneously to be inaccurate. Although we have reason to believe that this is not a problem, given our analysis of responses, we cannot entirely rule out the possibility that the VAM scores may be affecting our result.

2. *Too small a contrast between high- and low-performing teachers:* It is possible that the difference in VAM scores between the high- and low-performing groups of teachers may not have been large enough for judges to discriminate. All the teachers in the high-performing group had VAM scores that were *at least* 0.5 standard deviations above the district mean for 3 years. On the other hand, teachers in the low-performing group had VAM scores that were consistently *below* the district mean, not *0.5 standard deviations below* the mean. Thus, it is possible that judges were being asked to distinguish between pretty good teachers and very good teachers, which may have proved too subtle a distinction and one that did not correspond well to the labels "high-performing" and "low-performing."

3. *Inadequately trained judges:* Judges may have lacked the training—on a specific observation protocol or more broadly in education—that they needed in order to be accurate. This might have led judges to guess, apply criteria inconsistently, or rely on irrelevant criteria. These potential problems could have been heightened by selecting relatively small numbers of judges from heterogeneous groups. The relatively high agreement across raters, however, argues against guessing or the inconsistent use of criteria, while performing worse than chance suggests that their criteria were not only irrelevant but misleading. Nonetheless, a larger and better-trained group of judges might provide more accurate assessments.

4. *Non-representative video clips:* The video clips may not have represented the true instructional style of teachers for two reasons. First, given the small sample of teachers, it is possible that the randomization procedures, by chance, failed to produce a set of clips that were representative, thereby leading judges to appear more inaccurate than they were. The fact that teachers were selected at random from a pool of potential

subjects, that the researcher selecting the clips did not know the group affiliations of the teachers, that the clips were chosen according to the same procedures for each teacher, and that the clips were presented in random order, protect against systematic bias, but it does not rule out the possibility that a particular sample is biased. Second, although we can be confident from previous research that judgments made from short exposure to teaching behaviors are likely to correlate highly with judgments made from longer observations, it is possible that the clips were too short to be representative.

5. *Changes in the student population:* It is conceivable that the classes we filmed (comprised of students from the year of the study) were systematically different from the classes used to estimate value-added scores (comprised of students from the 3 years prior to the study). This in turn could have led teachers to adopt atypical styles of instruction or to be more or less effective with their new classes than they had been historically. Although there is no reason to believe that this was the case, it is possible, and it had the potential to make judges appear less accurate than they really were.

6. *Idiosyncratic local context:* For any number of reasons not described above, it is possible that our results accurately reflect the reality of the school district in which the experiment was conducted, but that the school district is so unusual that the results do not apply elsewhere. We have no reason to believe this is the case, but as with all experiments, replication is essential.

Experiment 2

In order to rule out some of the alternate explanations of Experiment 1, we replicated the experiment—with a number of intentional differences—using new samples of teachers, film clips, and judges. First, we selected teachers from a different district located in a different state, Tennessee (to help rule out Alternate Explanation 6). Second, we selected teachers based on a 3-year record of performing *at least* 0.50 standard deviations *above or below* the district mean value-added score (to help rule out Alternate Explanation 2), and calculated the scores in a way that was less prone to bias[24] (to help rule out Alternate Explanation 1). Then we filmed 20 4th- and 5th-grade teachers giving a lesson on fractions, and selected four above average and four below average for the experiment, based on the quality of the films and the similarity of the curriculum covered in the lesson (to help rule out Alternate Explanation 4). There were six female and two male teachers, most in the middle of their careers, one approaching retirement. In order to increase the chance of finding a relationship, we showed the clips to more judges (165) who all had expertise in education—school principals, assistant principals, and administrators-in-training—drawn both from Tennessee and California (to help rule out Alternate Explanation 3). The films were presented either in group format, or from a secure Web site via the Internet, using a proprietary software program requiring a unique password good for a single use. To confirm the accuracy of the group affiliations of the teachers, we checked their classes' achievements for the year of filming and found them to be consistent, in all eight cases, with their original standings derived from the historical data (to rule out Alternate Explanation 5).

This time we were interested only in inter-judge agreement, and accuracy. The patterns of inter-judge agreement among the administrators were similar to those found for judges in the first experiment. The correlations were 0.27 for individual and 0.98 for the group agreement, which were very close to those from Experiment 1. As before, agreement across teachers varied considerably, ranging from 60% to 88%.

As in Experiment 1, a simple count of correct assignments revealed that judges were not accurate. Judges classified from zero to seven teachers correctly, and the mean number correct, 3.85 out of 8, was slightly less than would be produced by chance. Accuracy again varied by teacher; two teachers, one high-performing and one-low performing, were accurately rated by over 80% of the administrators, while two other teachers were accurately rated by only 12% and 21% of the judges. Accuracy was not correlated with administrators' experience.

The results of Experiment 2 essentially replicated those from Experiment 1. With a more experienced and larger group of judges, a different set of teachers grouped more widely apart according to their records of achieving student achievement gains, and a more robust set of value-added calculations, we still saw a large degree of overall inter-judge agreement and accuracy that at best reflects chance.

These findings serve to strengthen the possibility that System 1 operations are overriding System 2 processes, even among school administrators who are likely to be experienced teacher evaluators. Furthermore, judges are responding to similar stimuli from the teaching behaviors, resulting in systematic (rather than random) evaluations that are not predictive of teacher effectiveness. However, certain teachers tend to be accurately identified by the majority of raters, suggesting that it might be possible to identify what it is about these teachers that aids judges and make use of that information in the development of a future measure. Other possible implications for the design of a measure that attempts to predict teacher effectiveness in student learning are that a) users need to be trained to employ System 2 rather than System 1 processes; b) the measure should consist only of items that reliably distinguish more effective from less effective teachers; c) and the measure should avoid items that trigger System 1 operations.

Experiment 3

As the next step in developing a more predictive measure, we replicated the experiment again, but with three important differences—judges were well trained, used an established observational measure, and viewed the full-length videos of teachers (from Experiment 2) presenting their lessons—in order to more completely rule out Alternate Explanations 3 and 4. We conducted this experiment in collaboration with researchers at the University of Virginia's Center for the Advanced Study of Teaching and Learning (CASTL), to whom we submitted the eight full-lesson films for ratings using the CLASS instrument, described in the previous chapter.[25] CLASS consists of 11 dimensions across three domains that cover *emotional support* (classroom climate, teacher sensitivity, regard for student perspectives), *classroom organization* (behavior management, productivity, instructional learning formats), and *instructional support* (concept development, quality of feedback, language modeling), and the fourth dimension of student engagement. The CLASS instrument is organized with student engagement as the dependent variable, and is believed to measure the effectiveness of teachers. (For technical information on the reliability and validity of CLASS, see the manual.[26]). Trained raters, ignorant to the value-added histories of the teachers (but aware that some were above and some below average), viewed and double-coded the eight lessons and scored them using the CLASS protocol. This produced a set of total scores that enabled a ranking of the teachers relative to each other. In order to assess accuracy, we allowed the scoring in the top half of the rankings to indicate above-average effectiveness, and in the bottom half below-average effectiveness. We also compared the CLASS ranks to those produced in Experiment 2, which were calculated according to the number of nominations a teacher received for being in the above-average group.

To everyone's surprise, judges using the CLASS protocol correctly categorized only 50% of the teachers. This result is indistinguishable from chance using any statistical test. Thus, even with training, a structured observational protocol, and access to the full lesson, CLASS judges only replicated the results of Experiment 2.

Although the overall CLASS scores did not successfully discriminate between the teachers in the above- and below-average groups, we wondered if certain items in the measure might consistently and accurately discriminate these groups. To investigate this, the trained scorers rated the lessons of the 12 teachers from Tennessee who were not included in Experiment 2, still ignorant as to their group affiliation. Then, after learning of the teachers' groupings, the raters did an item-by-item comparison of all 20 teachers divided into their two groups. This analysis showed that a small subset of items consistently produced scores that accurately identified teachers as either above or below average. All of these items were from the instructional domain. They included clear expression of the lesson objective, integrating students' prior knowledge, using opportunities to go beyond the current lesson, use of more than one delivery mechanism or modality, using multiple examples, giving feedback about process, and asking "how" and "why" questions.

The results from the CLASS ratings raise new questions and add weight to some of the possible interpretations of the findings from the first two experiments. Foremost, why would there be little difference between the ratings from Experiment 2 and Experiment 3? It may be that CLASS was not designed to be predictive of a teacher's value-added gains, per se, adopting an alternative and more expansive conception of good teaching. Furthermore, this conception may reflect a more formalized arrangement of the criteria used by judges in Experiments 1 and 2. CLASS is focused primarily on student engagement, and nearly two-thirds of its items gauge emotional support and classroom organization; the most commonly cited rating criteria in Experiment 1 was student engagement, followed by teaching strategies, teacher characteristics, and math knowledge. On the face of it, these appear to reflect very similar concerns. Yet the CLASS items that were identified as better predictors of teacher effectiveness came from the one-third that gauges instructional support. This suggests that emotional support and classroom organization may be highly valued and even necessary but not sufficient to ensure effective teaching. An instrument that is designed to predict student achievement would therefore do better to focus solely on the instructional items, which should yield low scores in classes where positive organization and climate are lacking, but not necessarily high scores when those features are well established.

Another possibility is that System 1 operations may influence judges even when they are trained to use a structured, rigorously developed instrument. Thus, it may not be enough just to have an instrument in hand, in contrast to the judges in Experiment 2 who had nothing; it may be necessary to train observers to be aware of and to factor out the many cognitive influences on judgments that result in errors, omissions, and inaccuracies.

Experiment 4

The fourth and last experiment involved testing the predictability of the new instrument that we developed out of the first three experiments. This new instrument, called the Rapid Assessment of Teacher Effectiveness consists of 11 items, all related to instruction, which are rated with a score of 1 (not present) to 3 (completely present). The 11 items are derived from the data collected in the first three experiments and include some refashioned elements from CLASS along with features associated with correct ratings from the 2-minute judges, and items derived from forensic comparisons of the films from the two groups of teachers by educational researchers. The text of the pilot version of the RATE follows.

Pilot Version of the Rapid Assessment of Teacher Effectiveness (RATE)

Teacher_____ Date_____ Grade _____
Subject_____
Lesson Topic _____
Introduction of new material _____ Middle of unit _____ Review _____

INDICATOR

1. **Lesson objective** is clearly expressed to students (posted or stated) and referred to regularly throughout the math lesson. May be seen when students are able to state in their own words what they are doing and why.

▶ The lesson objective, goal, SOL, or learning outcome is expressed verbally or visually. As the math lesson unfolds, teacher refers students to the objective as reinforcement. Students are conscious of the goal and are able to explain the purpose for the activities they are completing.

> 3 = All three elements are present: posted or verbal objective; reinforcement during lesson; students express goal or purpose
> 2 = Two elements present
> 1 = Objective is written or stated without reinforcement or student expression, or objective is absent or unclear
>
> **Score**_____

2. Teacher understands **student background** and comfort with material; integrates pre-assessment data, interests, prior knowledge; and presents material as attainable/doable.

▶ There is evidence of intentional/purposeful sequencing of instruction based on teacher knowledge of where students are in the instructional process and their understanding of the prerequisite material. He/she relates the current concepts to other material students have mastered. Students are told that they are able to reach the learning objective in a way that conveys confidence and support.

> 3 = All three elements are present: sequencing, integration/relation to prior knowledge; presentation inspires student confidence and support
> 2 = Only two elements present
> 1 = One or zero elements present, or teacher attempts at sequencing, relating to prior knowledge, or inspiring confidence are unsuccessful or poorly implemented
>
> **Score**_____

3. Teacher and/or students demonstrate consideration of the topic through **more than one delivery mechanism, perspective, modality, or learning style.**

▶ Teacher and/or students explore alternate ways to solve problems, view issues, or explain findings. May include use of discussion, written examples, kinesthetic activities, manipulatives, and audio-visual aids. Teacher capitalizes on his/her use of student learning preferences and interests.

(continued)

3 = Clearly successful implementation of use of more than one delivery mechanism, perspective, modality, or learning style

2 = Evidence of attempt on the part of the teacher or student to employ different delivery mechanism, etc., but not fully realized

1 = No evidence of this type of instruction

Score_____

4. Teacher provides/elicits from students **multiple examples** of the math concept being taught.

▶ In math, several problems of each type are presented.

3 = Teacher gives/elicits more than two examples for each variation of the math concept being taught

2 = Teacher does not give/elicit more than two examples for one or more variations of the math concept being taught

1 = Teacher never gives/elicits more than one or two examples for each variation of the math concept being taught

Score_____

5. Appropriate **non-examples** are given to students for comparison or teacher is able to explain why a student's contribution is not accurate.

▶ Teacher may intentionally offer non-examples or use "mistakes" to reinforce steps of a process and to clarify the learning objective. Teacher works with student(s) to reveal misconceptions when incorrect answers are offered.

3 = Teacher uses non-examples or mistakes in clarifying a concept; teacher regularly provides explanation or clarification for incorrect answers

2 = Teacher does one or other element from 3

1 = Teacher rarely or never uses non-examples and rarely or never explains incorrect answers

Score_____

6. The math concepts being taught are presented at a **pace** that is neither too slow, so that many students lose interest nor too fast so that many students do not understand.

3 = Teacher presents math concepts and material paced so that students always maintain interest and can understand

2 = Presentation is sometimes too fast or too slow

1 = Pacing is generally off-target

Score_____

7. Feedback to students is about **process** not just correctness--Asking why and how questions.

▶ Teacher does more than pronounce an answer as right or wrong. He/she asks questions that explore the thinking behind student responses. These may include questions such as "How did you come up with that answer?" or "Why is that?"

3 = Teacher provides exploratory feedback on the majority of occasions when it is possible

2 = Teacher occasionally provides exploratory feedback but not as often as he/she could

1 = Teacher rarely or never provides exploratory feedback

Score_____

8. Meaningful and timely opportunities for **guided practice** are provided. Examples include working with peers, work at the board, and supervised practice—anything where students get practice and immediate corrective feedback.

▶ Students are given an opportunity to wrestle with new learning in class, ask questions, get corrective feedback, and solidify knowledge before being asked to do work independently. This connects strongly with the need to provide students with clear steps in a skill-based process.

3 = Appropriate opportunities for guided practice are successfully and effectively implemented in the lesson

2 = Teacher provides opportunities for guided practice, but they are either not fully appropriate or are ineffectively implemented or both

1 = Teacher provides no opportunities for guided practice

Score_____

9.. Teacher uses language that describes and explains the math concepts being taught with **the clarity** that maximizes the likelihood that the students will understand.

▶ The teacher's language reflects both verbal ability and math knowledge such that explanations are clear and unambiguous and that all students are seen to be able to understand

3 = Teacher's explanations are clear, unambiguous and accessible to all students

2= Explanations sometimes lack clarity for at least some of the students

1 = Explanations are generally not clear enough for most students to understand

Score_____

10. Students are actively engaged throughout the lesson. Maximal time is spent on task.

▶ High engagement is when all students are actively involved in content activities that constitute most of the lesson period.

3 = All students are engaged in content work that covers the majority of the lesson

2 = Most students are engaged in content work that covers the majority of the lesson, or all students are engaged in content work but a significant portion of the lesson is off topic

1 = Many students are not engaged in content work, or most of the lesson is off topic

Score_____

TOTAL SCORE_____

Once the pilot instrument was drafted, two raters were trained to score films of complete math lessons. We conducted initial training using films of teachers from a different project. Raters practiced scoring, met to discuss scores and difficulties, and we recast the items where necessary to eliminate ambiguities and increase clarity before they scored more films. When both raters felt comfortable with the instrument and were achieving acceptable reliability, they rated the teachers from Experiment 3. Sixteen of the 20 films were usable—the eight from Experiment 2 plus eight more that had full lessons. Since the CLASS instrument uses 20-minute samples of teaching, films of incomplete lessons were acceptable for that measure. The RATE requires that raters view a complete lesson.

For this experiment, the two raters worked independently to score two or three teachers and then conferred to discuss their scores and reach consensus. After they completed all 16 sets of scores, we calculated the rater reliability and the correlation between their scores and the teachers' value-added groupings. Rater reliability was high: 0.86 for the individual ratings and 0.92 for the combined rating. For the predictability with the VAM scores, we used 9 of the 11 items in the measure. Items 3 and 5 were omitted from the analysis because scores were missing for some teachers. The items refer to elements that may not occur in every lesson. Scores on the remaining nine items were statistically significantly related to the value-added groupings of the teachers, correctly identifying 14 out of 16 teachers. An item analysis showed that certain items were more predictive than others, with item 10 correlating at 0.71 with value-added status, and items 8 and 7 correlating at 0.46 and 0.45.

With this relatively small sample, we should be cautious not to draw overconfident conclusions about the measure. The signs, however, are certainly promising that it has the ability to identify the teachers at the high and low end of the value-added continuum.

IMPLICATIONS

As I write this, our work to devise a new observational measure that correlates highly with student achievement gains is still in progress. What we have learned thus far is that, despite popular myth and a couple of research studies, school principals and others are not able, under experimental conditions, to identify correctly teachers whose students routinely achieve above or below average test gains. Furthermore, trained raters using an established valid and reliable classroom observation instrument were, in our study, no better than chance at classifying the higher- and lower-performing teachers. Certain cognitive operations that have been demonstrated to come into play when we make judgments of human behavior may be influencing these results. However, our new instrument, developed with learning from our experiments and with a sensitivity to cognitive operations, appears to be able to predict, with much better accuracy than found with other instruments, the effectiveness groupings of elementary math teachers. If, through further testing, we find that RATE continues to produce accurate predictions of value-added effectiveness, it has potential for use as an evaluation tool for principals to enable them to identify teachers who may benefit from extra support or who may be candidates for providing such support. Further testing will establish the validity of the instrument, and whether it is applicable to higher grade levels and, with some fine-tuning, for other school subjects. Although statisticians are improving the quality of VAM, it is still too early to rely on it as the only measure of a teacher's effectiveness. Of course, there is no reason why VAM cannot be applied to tests other than the state standardized tests that are used to measure school progress. Any valid and reliable test given to all students at the beginning and end of the school year can be used as a basis for calculating value-added scores. Ideally, a well-rounded teacher evaluation would include other elements that reflect teachers' contribution to the school, the community, and the profession.

6

Conclusion:
Implications from the Evidence

The widely held belief that the most important school factor for student learning is an effective teacher must unfortunately be juxtaposed with evidence that teaching no longer attracts the best and brightest university graduates, that teachers are poorly paid compared with other occupations, that we do not agree on what constitutes a high-quality teacher, and that we are not able to recognize an effective teacher when we see one.

Although we may applaud the increased professional opportunities for women since the 1960s, we must bemoan the fact that the intellectual quality of our K–12 teachers, who are still mostly women, has declined. As we welcome the proliferation of instruments for observing and evaluating classroom lessons along with the institutionalization of collecting student test data in a format that allows for the calculation of value-added scores, we must question the assumed relationship between teaching standards and student learning as well as the narrowness of the tests and the possible biases in the value-added models. It is not at all clear that the administrators who are responsible for evaluating our teachers are able to distinguish between those who are more or less effective, and it seems they end up assigning almost all teachers a satisfactory or better rating. It is doubly ironic that an organization like Teach for America *is* able to attract the best and brightest college graduates to serve as teachers in the most hard-to-staff schools, give them minimal preparation but still have them achieve positive results, only to see most of them quit after the required 2 years of service.

The research indicates that our present system uses the wrong criteria for assigning teachers' salary increases and tenure, by assuming that advanced degrees and years of experience are commensurate with producing more effective student learning. However, to use teacher value-added estimates as a basis for performance pay involves too many potential biases and is therefore a premature strategy.[1] My own research suggests that we may be able to use a combination of observation and value-added information to identify teachers at the two ends of the effectiveness spectrum and devise intervention strategies accordingly. We know we need to reform the accountability system. Many educators hold that accountability should be tied to effectiveness in increasing student learning. We are still debating how best to achieve this.

A considerable proportion of discretionary school district funds is spent on various forms of teacher professional development activities.[2] Although in-service training, mentoring, and continuing education are essential elements for maintaining high standards in any profession, such activities cannot fully negate the effects of having attracted underqualified teacher candidates in the first place. Although well-targeted professional development could certainly help raise the quality of our practicing teachers, it must be evaluated not solely in terms of how many hours a teacher attends workshops, but by the demonstrated effects it has on practice and subsequently on student learning.

Although a high-quality, effective teacher may be the single most important ingredient in a child's educational recipe, even the best teachers cannot perform successfully when certain school and societal factors act in opposition. One radical approach for dealing with this has been adopted by Geoffrey Canada with his project the Harlem Children's Zone (HCZ).[3] The HCZ addresses the negative educational effects of poverty by providing intense and wide-ranging support at the community level with outreach programs that start with neo-natal health care and continue until a child is in college. Such an approach requires considerable reallocation and addition of funds and may be difficult to institute everywhere. Even in Harlem, not all students win the lottery and make it into the HCZ schools.

As the United States falls in the global education rankings and American students compare less and less well with their foreign peers, especially in math and science, radical reform is needed in our K–12 school systems. At the heart of this reform must be the improvement in quality of the teaching workforce. To achieve this, we will need a more competitive salary structure together with better working conditions to attract higher-performing college graduates, effective in-service supports starting with induction, and solid methods for teacher evaluation that are empirically linked to student learning and attached to systems of accountability and promotion. However, not all reform must rest on the shoulders of the teachers. Perhaps it is time to radically rethink how we educate our children, incorporating all that technology and the Internet has to offer, moving from an agrarian-based school calendar, acknowledging that the best and brightest women now have other, more attractive professional opportunities, and addressing the social issues that work against the poor and the minorities, restricting their ability to participate equally in schooling with those who are more privileged.

It is the duty of the educational researcher to help educators move from data to information to action. Although we may not be able change society, we can provide assistance to those who can. An important start is to gain greater insight into what makes a teacher most effective, for teachers are at the heart of the matter.

Notes

Chapter 1

1. Dublin, 1983; Temin, 2002.

2. National Education Association, 2003.

3. The Schools and Staffing Survey (SASS) is operated by the National Center for Education Statistics (NCES), a part of the federal government's Department of Education, Institute of Education Sciences. A detailed description is available at http://nces.ed.gov/surveys/sass/.

4. Ingersoll & Merrill, 2010.

5. Corcoran, Evans, & Schwab, 2004.

6. Murnane, Singer, Willett, Kemple, & Olsen, 1991.

7. Manski, 1985.

8. Corcoran, Evans, & Schwab, 2004.

9. School teaching was formally designated a profession in Malta by the British Education Reform Act of 1988. In the United States, it is now generally considered advanced in its process of professionalization. For a thorough discussion of the professionalization of teaching, see Ingersoll and Perda, 2008. Also relevant is Wise, 2005.

10. Bacolod, 2007, p. 737.

11. Data taken from Bacolod, 2005, p. 742.

12. The NLS Original Cohort (YM, YW) geocode data may be accessed only at a Census Regional Data Center, and thus subject to the Census Bureau's procedures for access to Title 13 data. The Bureau of Labor Statistics handles applications for access to the NLS-Y79 geocode data.

13. High scoring is defined as scoring above 80th percentile on IQ, measured by the Armed Forces Qualifying Test (AFQT)

14. Murnane et al., 1991.

15. U.S. Department of Education, 1997.

16. Ingersoll & Merrill, 2010.

17. Barron's Educational Series, 2009.

18. Bee & Dolton, 1995; Hanushek & Rivkin, 1997; Lakdawalla, 2001.

19. Lakdawalla, 2006.

20. Lakdawalla, 2006, p. 321.

21. AFT, 2008.

22. Podgursky, 2003.

23. Blau & Duncan 1967; Hodge, Siegel, & Rossi 1964; Hodge, Treiman, & Rossi 1966; Treiman, 1977.

24. Counts, 1925, p. 17.

25. The scores are derived from analysis of the interview responses whereby participants were asked to rank occupational titles using a 9-rung ladder (see Nakao & Treas, 1990).

26. Hargreaves et al., 2006.

27. Hargreaves et al., 2006, p. 60.

28. Smith, 2007.

29. E.g., Aaronson, Barrow, & Sander, 2007; Goldhaber & Brewer, 2000; Hanushek, 1992; Kane et al., 2008; Nye, Konstantopoulos, & Hedges, 2004; Rivkin, Hanushek, & Kain, 2005; Sanders, 2000.

30. Hanushek, 2010.

31. Coleman et al., 1966.

32. Eide, Goldhaber, & Brewer, 2004.

33. See e.g., Goldhaber & Brewer, 2000, and Walsh, 2001.

34. Hargreaves & Goodson, in Goodson & Hargreaves, 1996, p. 4.

35. Hoyle, 2008, p. 285.

36. Etzioni, 1969, Preface, p. v.

37. Hargreaves, 2000, p. 153.

38. In 2004, Mathematica Policy Associates published a randomized control study comparing Teach for America teachers with a control group of traditionally certified teachers. They found that Teach for America attracted higher proportions of graduates from top-tier colleges, and that their students made greater gains in math than those of control teachers, and were no different in reading (Decker, Mayer, & Glazerman, 2004).

39. Darling-Hammond, 1990, 1996.

40. Ballou & Podgursky, 1993.

41. See e.g., Goldhaber, 2002; Murnane & Cohen, 1986.

42. Glazerman, Goldhaber, Loeb, Staiger, & Whitehurst, 2010.

43. The NEA position may be viewed in full at http://www.nea.org/home/36780.htm.

Chapter 2

1. This quote from an interview with Charlie Rose was cited by Chait (2009):

> "One piece of No Child Left Behind calls for highly qualified teachers, but those qualifications are . . . front-end qualifications—does the person have this certificate or this degree? And I believe we have to move away from the front-end inputs to looking at highly effective teachers. If you can produce results in the classroom, that makes you effective, and you can stay in the classroom. And it really shouldn't matter whether or not you have your Ph.D. or your master's."

2. Berliner (2005). He cites data from the National Assessment of Educational Progress (NAEP), which demonstrates growth for all racial and ethnic groups among 9-, 13-, and 17-year-olds in all three of the subject areas regularly tested: reading, mathematics, and science.

3. Blanton, Sindelar, Correa, Hardman, McDonnell, & Kuhel, 2003.

4. Witty, 1947, p. 662.

5. E.g., Murray, 1983; Soar & Soar, 1979; Sparks & Lipka, 1992.

6. Walker, 2008.

7. Lasley, 1980; Walls, Nardi, von Minden, & Hoffman, 2002; Witcher, Onwuegbuzie, & Minor, 2001;

8. Tabachnick & Zeichner, 1984.

9. Brown, Morehead, & Smith, 2008.

10. Hyland, 1996, p. 168.

11. Maslow, 1968; Rogers, 1969.

12. See, e.g., Combs, Blume, Newman, & Wass, 1974.

13. Tickle, 1999.

14. Korthagen, 2004.

15. Rosch, 1973, 1978.

16. Sternberg & Horvath, 1995, p. 10.

17. Sternberg & Horvath, 1995, p.14

18. The American Association for the Advancement of Science (AAAS), 1993 (the AAAS was created in 1848. Its goals are to promote cooperation among scientists, defend scientific freedom, encourage scientific responsibility, and support scientific education and science outreach "for the betterment of all humanity." It is the world's largest general scientific society, and publisher of the well-known scientific journal *Science);* The National Council of Teachers of Mathematics (NCTM), 1989, 1991, 2000 (the NCTM was founded in 1920. It publishes journals and holds conferences and is highly influential in directing math education in the United States); The National Research Council (NRC), 1996 (the NRC was established in 1916, and is the working arm of the U.S. National Academy of Sciences and the U.S. National Academy of Engineering, and conducts most studies done in their names).

19. NCTM, 1989, 2000.

20. NCTM, 1991.

21. See Schoenfeld, 2004, for a good account of the history of the math wars.

22. Fenstermacher & Richardson, 2005.

23. Fenstermacher & Richardson, 2005, p. 209.

24. Value-added models have two key features. First, the dependent variables in the analysis are designed to measure the amount of change that occurs in students' achievement during the year when students are in the classrooms under study. Second, measures of change are adjusted for differences across classrooms in students' prior achievement, home and social background (in some versions), and the social composition of the schools that students attended. The purpose of value-added models is to estimate the proportions of variance in changes in student achievement attributable to classrooms (i.e., teachers), after controlling for the effects of other, confounding variables.

25. E.g., Skinner & Belmont, 1993.

26. E.g., Fetler, 1997.

27. E.g., Webster & Mendro, 1995.

28. Campbell,Kyriakides, Muijis, & Robinson, 2003.

29. E.g., Carlgren, 1999.

30. Muijs, Campbell, Kyriakides, & Robinson, 2005.

Chapter 3

1. Darling-Hammond & Youngs, 2002; Goe, 2007; Rice, 2003; Wayne & Youngs, 2003; Wilson & Floden, 2003.

2. Wilson & Floden, 2003; Wilson, Floden & Ferrini-Mundy, 2001.

3. Goldhaber & Brewer, 2000.

4. Jepsen & Rivkin, 2002.

5. Betts, Zau, & Rice, 2003.

6. Hawk, Coble, & Swanson, 1985.

7. Cavalluzzo, 2004.

8. Darling-Hammond, Holtzman, Gatlin, & Heilig, 2005.

9. Kane, Rockoff, & Staiger, 2008.

10. National Board Certification is offered by the National Board for Professional Teaching Standards (NBPTS). The assessment process for National Board Certification requires candidates to complete two major components: a portfolio of classroom practice including samples of student work and videotapes of teacher instruction, and an assessment of content knowledge administered at a computer-based testing center. The process takes the better part of a school year and may involve 200–400 hours of work outside of the classroom.

11. Goldhaber & Anthony, 2007.

12. Clotfelter, Ladd, & Vigdor, 2007a, 2007b, 2007c.

13. McColskey et al., 2006.

14. McColskey et al., 2006, p. 95.

15. Sanders, Ashton, & Wright, 2005.

16. Harris & Sass, 2009.

17. Monk, 1994. Note: Wayne and Youngs (2003) exclude Monk's study from their review because he did not control for socioeconomic status.

18. Wenglinsky, 2000, 2002.

19. Anita Summers is the mother of Lawrence Summers, who is currently director of the White House's National Economic Council for President Barack Obama, and is mentioned as having contributed to the paper referenced here.

20. Summers & Wolfe, 1977, p. 644.

21. Clotfelter et al., 2007a, p. 28.

22. *High School and Beyond* is a large-scale longitudinal study conducted by the National Opinion Research Center in 1980 under contract with the National Center for Education Statistics. It used a stratified national probability sample of more than 1,100 secondary schools, with up to 36 sophomores and 36 seniors initially interviewed from each school in the spring of

1980. More than 30,000 sophomores and 28,000 seniors participated in the base-year interviews. Ehrenberg and Brewer's (1994) study focused on the sophomores, who were given tests in mathematics, vocabulary, and reading.

23. Ehrenberg & Brewer, 1994, p. 1 (Abstract).

24. Aaronson, Barrow, & Sander, 2007, p. 129.

25. NELS:88 surveyed a nationally representative sample of 8th-graders first in the spring of 1988. A sub-sample of these respondents was then resurveyed through four follow-ups in 1990, 1992, 1994, and 2000. On the questionnaire, students reported on a range of topics, including school, work, and home experiences; educational resources and support; the role in education of their parents and peers; neighborhood characteristics; educational and occupational aspirations; and other student perceptions. Additional topics included self-reports on smoking, alcohol and drug use, and extracurricular activities. For the three in-school waves of data collection (when most were 8th-graders, sophomores, or seniors), achievement tests in reading, social studies, mathematics, and science were administered in addition to the student questionnaire (from the NCES Web site: http://nces.ed.gov/surveys/NELS88/). Therefore, the NELS:88 follow-up datasets permit longitudinal analyses of growth in student achievement from 8th to 10th grade, 10th to 12th grade, and 8th to 12th grade in particular subjects.

26. Goldhaber & Brewer, 1997.

27. Betts et al., 2003.

28. Carr, 2006 (for teachers in traditional public schools); Clotfelter, Ladd, & Vigdor, 2006; Harris & Sass, 2009.

29. Carr, 2006 (for teachers in charter schools); Hanushek, Kain, O'Brien, & Rivkin, 2005; Harris & Sass, 2009.

30. Fenstermacher, 1990.

31. NCAC Web site: http://www.teach-now.org/frmOverviewOfATC1.asp

32. Decker, Mayer, & Glazerman, 2004.

33. Darling-Hammond, 1997, p.310.

34. Darling-Hammond, 2002, pp. 12–13.

35. Laczko-Kerr & Berliner, 2002.

36. Laczko-Kerr & Berliner, 2002.

37. Kane, Rockoff & Staiger., 2008.

38. Kane et al., 2008, p. 629.

39. Boyd, Grossman, Lankford, Loeb, & Wyckoff, 2006.

40. E.g. Walsh & Jacobs, 2007, found that among 49 alternative certification programs in 11 states, two-thirds accepted half or more of their applicants, and one-quarter accepted virtually everyone who applied. Only four in ten programs required a college GPA of 2.75 or above.

41. Constantine et al., 2009.

42. Corcoran & Jennings, 2009.

43. Corcoran & Jennings, 2009, summary.

44. Murnane & Philips, 1981(b).

45. Hanushek, 1992.

46. Ferguson & Brown, 2000, p. 138.

47. Hanushek & Rivkin, 2006.

48. Clotfelter et al., 2006.

49. Harris & Sass, 2008.

50. Pedagogical content knowledge was first proposed by Shulman (1986) and developed with colleagues in the Knowledge Growth in Teaching project as a broader perspective model for understanding teaching and learning. This project studied how novice teachers acquired new understandings of their content, and how these new understandings influenced their teaching. Shulman described pedagogical content knowledge as the knowledge formed by the synthesis of three knowledge bases: subject-matter knowledge, pedagogical knowledge, and knowledge of context. Pedagogical content knowledge was unique to teachers and separated, for example, a math teacher from a mathematician.

51. Hill, Rowan, & Ball, 2005.

52. Rowan, Chiang, & Miller, 1997.

53. Betts et al., 2003, p. 89.

54. Harris & Sass, 2008.

55. Monk, 1994.

56. Cohen & Hill, 2000.

57. Wenglinksy, 2000, 2002.

58. Kannapel & Clements, 2005.

59. Harbison & Hanushek, 1992.

60. Murnane, 1975.

61. This study was mandated by Congress as part of the government's evaluation of the Title 1 program.

62. Rowan, Correnti, & Miller, 2002.

63. Cavalluzzo, 2004.

64. Rockoff, 2004, p. 247.

65. Hanushek, 1971.

66. The Buckeye Institute for Public Policy Solutions is a nonprofit, conservative, and libertarian research organization. Its stated mission is to promote individual liberty, economic freedom, personal responsibility, and limited government in the state of Ohio. Its operating philosophy states: "Free markets enable free men and women to find prosperity." The institute's Center for Education Excellence produces reports and research that promote a market-based approach to education, including vouchers and charter schools, and a resolution to the state's years-old education funding debate. It is often at odds with the teacher unions.

67. Gallagher, 2004.

68. Carr, 2006, p. 10.

69. E.g., Hanushek, 1996, 1997, 2003; Hanushek & Rivkin, 2004; Hanushek, Rivkin, Rothstein, & Podgurksy, 2004.

70. Hanushek & Rivkin, 2006.

71. NCTAF, 1996.

72. NCTAF, 1996, pp. 15–16.

73. According to its Web site, the Abell Foundation is a philanthropic institution that provides grants to schools, hospitals, and human service organizations to cater to the needs of disadvantaged residents of Baltimore and its surroundings.

74. The National Council on Teacher Quality (NCTQ) is a research and advocacy group that describes itself as being "dedicated to increasing the accountability and transparency" of states and district preparation programs "which have the greatest influence on teacher quality." (From the testimony of Sandi Jacobs, Vice President for Policy at NCTQ, at a DC Board of Education hearing on December 10, 2008; available at: http://sboe.dc.gov/sboe/lib/sboe/Sandi_Jacobs.pdf.)

75. See Darling-Hammond, 2001, 2002; Walsh 2001, 2002; Walsh & Podgursky, 2001.

76. Darling-Hammond, Berry, & Thoreson, 2001; Goldhaber & Brewer, 2000.

77. Darling-Hammond et al., 2005.

78. See Case 3:07-cv-04299-PJH, document 76, filed 6/17/2008, U.S. District Court of Northern California.

79. E.g., Clewell & Villegas, 1998; Graham, 1987; NCTAF, 1996; U.S. Department of Education, 1997.

80. Dee 2004, 2005.

81. Dee, 2005.

82. Dee, 2004.

83. Hanushek et al., 2005.

84. Rosenthal & Jacobson, 1968a, 1968b.

85. Ferguson, 2003.

86. See, e.g., Baron, Tom, & Cooper, 1985.

87. Ehrenberg, Goldhaber, & Brewer, 1995.

88. The NLSY is a panel dataset of about 12,000 respondents aged 14–22, conducted in 1979. It included questions on the percentage of female faculty and professional staff in addition to other questions about salary, advanced degrees, ethnicity, faculty-student ratio, student gender percentages, and percentage of students classified as disadvantaged.

89. Nixon & Robinson, 1999.

90. Getzels & Jackson, 1963.

91. The MBTI is a Jungian-based self-report psychological inventory designed to determine personality characteristics and learning styles. It consists of 166 items that relate to four separate scales: Extraversion/Introversion; Sensing/Intuition; Thinking/Feeling; Judging/Perceiving.

92. Rushton, Morgan, & Richard, 2007.

93. The term *locus of control* has been interpreted as representing the extent to which teachers could control the reinforcement of their actions. See, e.g., Rotter, 1990.

94. For Bandura, *self-efficacy* was the outcome of a cognitive process in which people construct beliefs about their capacity to perform at a given level of competence. See, e.g., Bandura, 1982.

95. Goddard, Hoy, & Hoy, 2000.

96. E.g., Armor et al., 1976; Berman & McLaughlin, 1977.

97. E.g., Ashton & Webb, 1986; Ashton, Webb, & Doda, 1983; Rosenholtz, 1989.

98. McColsky et al., 2006.

99. Goddard, Hoy, & Hoy, 2000.

100. E.g., Allinder, 1994.

101. Rosenthal & Jacobson, 1968a.

102. Snow, 1969.

103. Thorndike, 1968.

104. Snow, 1969.

105. Jussim & Harber, 2005.

106. E.g., Hofer, 1994; Jones, 1986; Rist, 1970; Taylor, 1992; Weinstein & McKown, 1998.

107. E.g., Braun, 1976; Brophy & Good, 1974; Cooper, 1979; Dusek, 1975; Elashoff & Snow, 1971; Finn, 1972; Good, 1981; Raudenbush, 1984, 1994; Snow, 1969, 1995; Spitz, 1999; West & Anderson, 1976; Wineburg, 1987.

108. Merton, 1948, 1968, p. 477.

109. W. I. Thomas stated in 1928 that "If men define situations as real, they are real in their consequences." Thomas & Thomas, 1928.

110. Merton, 1968, p. 477.

111. E.g., Rist, 1970; Smith, Jussim, & Eccles, 1999; West & Anderson, 1976.

112. E.g., Jussim, Eccles, & Madon, 1996; Madon, Jussim, & Eccles, 1997.

113. Jussim & Harber, 2005.

114. U.S. Department of Education, 2002, pp. 39–40.

115. Coleman et al., 1966.

116. Ferguson, 1991.

117. Darling-Hammond & Youngs, 2002.

118. Andrew, Cobb, & Giampietro, 2005.

119. Ehrenberg & Brewer, 1995.

120. Ehrenberg & Brewer, 1994, p. 14.

121. Andrew, Cobb, & Giampietro, 2005.

122. Wayne & Youngs, 2003, p. 100.

123. Danielson, 2007.

124. Heneman, Milanowski, Kimball, & Odden, 2006.

125. Borman & Kimball, 2005.

126. Kimball, White, Milanowski, & Borman, 2004.

127. Holtzapple, 2003.

128. Gallagher, 2004.

129. Milanowski, 2004.

130. Matsumura et al., 2006.

131. Schachter & Thum, 2004.

132. Jacob & Lefgren, 2008.

133. The audit process involved a six-member team, including a teacher intervention specialist, teacher, district and building administrators, parent, and teacher educator, visiting each school for a week. In addition to classroom observations, they conducted interviews and reviewed school documents.

134. Kannapel & Clements, 2005.

135. See California Department of Education, 1985.

136. For a full description of the NCTM standards, visit http://standards.nctm.org/document/appendix/numb.htm. The overview on their Web site is as follows: "The Standards for school mathematics describe the mathematical understanding, knowledge, and skills that students should acquire from prekindergarten through grade 12. Each Standard consists of two to four specific goals that apply across all the grades. For the five Content Standards, each goal encompasses as many as seven specific expectations for the four grade bands considered in Principles and Standards: prekindergarten through grade 2, grades 3–5, grades 6–8, and grades 9–12. For each of the five Process Standards, the goals are described through examples that demonstrate what the Standard should look like in a grade band and what the teacher's role should be in achieving the Standard. Although each of these Standards applies to all grades, the relative emphasis on particular Standards will vary across the grade bands."

137. Cohen & Hill, 2000.

138. This is a description of NAEP from the Department of Education Web site: "The National Assessment of Educational Progress (NAEP) is the largest nationally representative and continuing assessment of what America's students know and can do in various subject areas. Assessments are conducted periodically in mathematics, reading, science, writing, the arts, civics, economics, geography, and U.S. history.

Since NAEP assessments are administered uniformly using the same sets of test booklets across the nation, NAEP results serve as a common metric for all states and selected urban districts. The assessment stays essentially the same from year to year, with only carefully documented changes. This permits NAEP to provide a clear picture of student academic progress over time."

139. Machin & McNally, 2008.

140. Machin and McNally describe the literacy hour as follows: "Key components of the policy are a framework for teaching, which sets out termly teaching objectives for the 5–11 age range and provides a practical structure of time and class management for a daily literacy hour. With regard to the former, a range of texts are specified and teaching objectives are set out at three levels (text, sentence and word) to match the text types studied. The daily literacy hour is divided between 10–15 minutes of whole-class reading or writing; 10–15 minutes whole-class session on word work (phonics, spelling and vocabulary) and sentence work (grammar and punctuation); 25–30 minutes of directed group activities (on aspects of writing or reading); and a plenary session at the end for pupils to revisit the objectives of the lesson, reflect on what they have learnt and consider what they need to do next." (p. 1444).

141. See Beard, 2000; Scheerens, 1992.

142. Schwerdt & Wuppermann, 2009.

143. National Council for the Teaching of Mathematics, 1991; National Research Council, 1996.

144. TIMSS is a survey conducted every 4 years among 4th- and 8th-grade students of mathematics and science. It started in 1995. In 2003, about 50 countries participated. A subsequent survey in 2007 covered 59 countries, and the next survey in 2011 will have 68. Its goal,

as stated on the TIMSS Web site, is to "conduct comprehensive state-of the-art assessments of student achievement supported with extensive data about country, school, and classroom learning environments. . . . There is enormous diversity among the TIMSS countries—in terms of economic development, geographical location, and population size. Fundamental to IEA's vision is the notion that the diversity of educational philosophies, models, and approaches that characterize the world's education systems constitute a natural laboratory in which each country can learn from the experiences of others. TIMSS participants share the conviction that comparing education systems in terms of their organization, curricula, and instructional practices in relation to their corresponding student achievement provides information crucial for effective education policy-making."

145. Aslam & Kingdon, 2007.

146. Frome et al., 2005.

147. Marcoulides, Heck, & Papanastasiou, 2005, p. 146.

148. See Chapter 2, note 21.

149. Goldhaber & Hansen, 2010.

150. The reader may recall that the purpose of a Value Added Model (VAM) is to estimate the proportions of variance in changes in student achievement attributable to classrooms (i.e., teachers), after controlling for the effects of other, confounding variables.

151. Aaronson, Barrow, & Sander, 2007, p. 97.

152. Rivkin, Hanushek, & Kain, 2005.

153. Rockoff, 2004.

154. Noell & Burns, 2006.

155. Nye, Konstantopoulos, & Hedges, 2004.

156. The Tennessee Class Size Experiment or Project STAR (Student Teacher Achievement Ratio) was an experiment that involved students in 79 elementary schools in 42 school districts in Tennessee. Within each school, kindergarten students were randomly assigned to classrooms in one of three treatment conditions: small classes (with 13 to 17 students), larger classes (with 22 to 26 students), or larger classes with a full-time classroom aide. Teachers were also randomly assigned to classes of different types that were maintained through the 3rd grade. Some students entered the study in the 1st grade and subsequent grades, but were randomly assigned to classes at that time. Teachers at each subsequent grade level were randomly assigned to classes as the experimental cohort passed through its grade. Districts had to agree to participate for 4 years, allow site visitations for verification of class sizes, interviewing, and data collection, including extra student testing. They also had to allow the research staff to randomly assign pupils and teachers to class types and to maintain the assignment of students to class types from kindergarten through grade 3. Since the classes within each school are initially equivalent (due to random assignment), any systematic differences in achievement among classes must be due to one of two sources: the treatment or differences in teacher effectiveness. Thus, within a school, any systematic variance in achievement between classrooms that had the same treatment must be due to variations in teacher effectiveness.

157. Falch, Song, & Smith, 2010.

158. McNeil, 2007.

Chapter 4

1. Founded in 1954, NCATE accredits teacher certification programs at colleges and universities in the United States.

2. NBTS is a body that provides an advanced k-12 teaching credential to US teachers who voluntarily submit to 10 assessments reviewed by a board of trained teachers from their areas.

3. According to the American Federation of Teachers (AFT) report in 2001, 29 states plus the District of Columbia had developed teaching standards in the core subject areas of English, mathematics, social studies, and science for elementary, middle, and high schools (AFT, 2001, p. 5).

4. See Cohen, 2010, for a full exposition of this issue.

5. See Brophy, 1986; Brophy & Good, 1986; Good, 1983.

6. Cohen, 2010, p. 383.

7. Carnegie Task Force on Teaching, Carnegie Corporation, 1986; National Commission on Excellence in Education, 1983.

8. Cohen, 2010, p. 386.

9. Validity theory is a complex area of study. For some key sources the reader is referred to Cronbach, 1971, 1988; Kane, 2006; Messick, 1989; Sireci, 2007.

10. A useful guide to teacher evaluation instruments is available through the National Comprehensive Center for Teacher Quality at http://www3.learningpt.org/tqsource/GEP/GEPEval-Type.aspx?tid = 1

11. *Praxis III* is a classroom assessment system that measures the classroom performance and teaching abilities of teachers in their first 2 years of teaching. As described on the ETS Web site, the assessment covers "organizing content for student learning (teaching planning), professional responsibilities, creating an environment for learning (classroom environment), and instruction." The Web site further states: "The PRAXIS III cannot be used to make employment decisions about currently licensed teachers. However, a poor PRAXIS III assessment can leave a blot on your record as an educator."

12. A constructivist approach to teaching and learning is based on the notion that students learn by fitting new information with what they already know to construct new knowledge. This process is affected by the context in which knowledge is imparted as well as by the beliefs and attitudes of the students.

13. For information about this project, see: http://www.metproject.org/

14. Heneman et al., 2006.

15. Kane et al., 2010.

16. Pianta, La Paro, & Hamre, 2008.

17. Pianta, La Paro, Payne, Cox, & Bradley, 2002.

18. NICHD ECCRN, 2002.

19. Hamre & Pianta, 2005.

20. Mashburn et al., 2008.

21. Howes et al., 2008.

22. LoCasale-Couch et al., 2007; Pakarinen et al., 2010; Rimm-Kaufman, La Paro, Downer, & Pianta, 2005.

23. See http://cset.stanford.edu/research/tools.html

24. Grossman et al., 2010.

25. Grossman et al., 2010, p. 27.

26. Hill et al., 2008, abstract.

27. Learning Mathematics for Teaching, 2006.

28. Hill et al., 2008, p. 441.

29. Hill, Umland, & Kapitula, 2010.

30. Schachter & Thum, 2004.

31. Goldhaber & Anthony, 2007.

32. Brandt, Mathers, Oliva, Brown-Sims, & Hess, 2007.

33. See, e.g., Downey, Steffy, English, Frase, & Poston, 2004.

34. Brandt et al., 2007.

35. See Bommer, Johnson, Rich, Podsakoff, & MacKenzie, 1995; and Heneman, 1986, for reviews and meta-analyses.

36. Alexander & Wilkins, 1982.

37. Jacob & Lefgren, 2008, p. 104 (footnote 5).

38. Murnane, 1975.

39. Harris & Sass, 2007.

40. Medley & Coker, 1987, p. 243.

41. Jacob & Lefgren, 2008.

42. Jacob & Lefgren, 2008, p. 130.

43. Harris, 2009.

44. Harris & Sass, 2007.

45. Wilkerson, Manatt, Rogers, & Maughan, 2000.

46. The New Teacher Project, 2007.

47. See the NBPTS Web site at http://www.nbpts.org/for_candidates/the_portfolio

48. Ballou, 2003.

49. See, e.g., Tucker, Stronge, Gareis, & Beers, 2003.

50. Clare & Aschbacher, 2001.

51. Newmann and Associates, 1996; Newmann, Marks, & Gamoran, 1996.

52. Silver, Mesa, Morris, Star, & Benken, 2009.

53. Silver et al., p. 501, abstract.

54. Borko et al., 2005, 2006, 2007; Stecher et al., 2005.

55. Borko et al., 2005, p. 99.

56. E.g., Jones & Swanson, 2009.

57. Burstein et al., 1995.

58. See the project's Web site (www.sii.soe.umich.edu) as well as the following papers: Camburn & Barnes, 2004; Correnti, 2007; Correnti & Rowan, 2007; Rowan, Correnti, Miller, & Camburn, 2009; Rowan, Camburn, & Correnti, 2004; Rowan & Miller, 2007.

59. Rowan & Correnti, 2009.

60. Camburn & Han, 2006.

61. Camburn & Barnes, 2004.

62. Rowan & Correnti, 2009.

63. Rowan & Correnti, p. 126.

64. Mayer, 1999.

65. NCTM, 1989.

66. For one review, see Wachtel, 1998.

67. Follman, 1992, 1995.

68. Sanders & Rivers, 1996; Wright, Horn, & Sanders, 1997.

69. The *LA Times* story can be accessed at http://www.latimes.com/news/local/teachers-investigation/

70. E.g., Baker et al., 2010; Braun, Chudowsky, & Koenig, 2010; Newton, Darling-Hammond, Haertel, & Thomas, 2010; a special issue of *Education Finance and Policy*, Fall 2009, Volume 4, Issue 4.

71. Braun et al., 2010.

72. Ballou, 2009.

73. Sanders & Horn, 1998.

74. Ballou, Sanders, & Wright, 2004.

75. Amrein-Beardsley, 2008; Kupermintz, 2003; McCaffrey, Lockwood, Koretz, Louis, & Hamilton, 2004.

76. Ray, McCormack, & Evans, 2009.

77. Wright, 2008.

78. Harris, 2009.

79. McCaffrey, Sass, Lockwood, & Mihaly, 2009; Newton et al., 2010.

80. Koedel & Betts, 2007; Lockwood, McCaffrey, Hamilton, Stecher, Le, & Martinez, 2007.

81. McCaffrey, Han, & Lockwood, 2008.

82. McCaffrey, Han, & Lockwood, 2009.

83. Goldhaber & Hansen, 2010.

84. Goldhaber & Hansen, 2010, p. 30.

85. Dee, 2004, 2005.

86. Campbell et al., 2003; 2004.

87. Weisberg, Sexton, Mulhern, & Keeling, 2009.

88. See Pecheone & Wei, 2009, for a critique of "The Widget Effect." They find fault with the study's absence of information about sampling procedures and survey response rates, and with its failure to take into account other "promising" teacher evaluation strategies.

89. See the Baker et al., 2010, report as an example.

90. One forum was held at UC–Berkeley on September 27, 2010, and broadcast over the Internet. Panel presentations included statements from statisticians, journalists, policy specialists, and educators. It is archived at http://gse.berkeley.edu/admin/events/gradingtheteachers.html

91. Dillon, 2010.

92. Sanders, 2000.

Chapter 5

1. See Strong, Gargani, & Hacifazlioğlu, (2011) for an expanded and more technical account of the first three experiments.

2. Strong, 2009.

3. E.g., Wason, 1960.

4. Kunda, 1990.

5. Mack & Rock, 1998; Simons & Chabris, 1999.

6. See Miller, 1956, for the classic paper on channel capacity.

7. Ross, Lepper, & Hubbard, 1975.

8. E.g., Davis, Lohse, & Kottemann, 1994.

9. E.g., Christensen-Szalanski, 1991; Fischhoff, 2001; Hawkins & Hastie, 1990.

10. E.g., James, 1890/1950; Johnson-Laird, 1983; Neisser, 1963; Piaget, 1926; Vygotsky, 1934/1987.

11. E.g., Chaiken & Trope, 1999; Epstein, 1994; Kahneman & Frederick, 2002; Sloman, 1996.

12. Stanovich & West, 2000.

13. Kahneman & Frederick, 2005.

14. Frederick, 2005.

15. Kahneman, 2002.

16. Ambady & Gray, 2002.

17. For a review, see Ambady, Bernieri, & Richeson, 2000.

18. Ambady & Rosenthal, 1992.

19. Benjamin & Shapiro, 2009.

20. Downey et al., 2004.

21. Calculation of teacher value-added scores from the student achievement data was done using a regression equation that included student and class characteristics. The analysis was guided by Sanders's work (Sanders & Horn, 1995) on value-added models in that we used the previous year's student achievement test score to predict the current year's score. We chose to use a simple regression equation to analyze the data. A conceptual description of the regression equation can be written as:

Current Score = Constant + Previous Score+ Student Factors + Class Factors + School/External Factors

For this analysis, we defined *Student Factors* in terms of a student's minority and poverty status. Student minority status is defined as 1 if a student is an ethnic minority, or 0 if Caucasian. Student poverty level is 1 if a student participates in the free/reduced-cost lunch program and 0 if not. *Class Factors* include the proportion of students in a class who are minority status, who are receiving free/reduced-cost lunch, and the class's level of prior achievement. We also included a dummy variable for school in the equation as a way of separating out school and district level variance. We recognize that this method of calculating value-added scores has been criticized for yielding biased estimates. It is a limitation of this part of the study that we addressed in second and third experiments.

22. We recognize that activity structures other than direct instruction exist and are often preferred. However, we chose to use examples of direct instruction for the experiment because it was easier to standardize across teachers, and guaranteed that raters would see a teacher interacting with the whole class with a range of behaviors that included explaining concepts, fielding questions, giving and eliciting examples, and so on.

23. McCaffrey, Han, & Lockwood, 2009.

24. Value-added scores were provided to us by the school district, which, as do all districts in the state, receives its value-added scores from William Sanders and the SAS Institute in North Carolina. This quote from the SAS Web site describes his approach to calculating value-added scores:

"To accommodate the technical requirements of a mixed-model application of the scope of SAS EVAAS, Sanders and his colleagues have developed a software system capable of solving thousands of equations iteratively. This complex system enables a massive multivariate, longitudinal analysis using all achievement data for each student, even those with incomplete testing histories, to estimate the effects of teachers, schools and school systems. The development of this software has allowed the inherent advantages of longitudinal analyses to be extended to a statewide application, previously unavailable from commercial software. Compared to simpler approaches to educational value-added assessment, the SAS EVAAS system offers a number of advantages."

25. Pianta, La Paro, & Hamre. 2008.

26. Pianta, La Paro, & Hamre, 2008.

Chapter 6

1. Rivkin, 2009.

2. Rice, 2009.

3. See http://www.hcz.org/

References

Aaronson, D., Barrow, L., & Sander, W. (2007). Teachers and student achievement in the Chicago public high schools. *Journal of Labor Economics, 25*(1), 95–135.

Alexander, E. R., & Wilkins, R. D. (1982). Performance rating validity: The relationship of objective and subjective measures of performance. *Group and Organization Studies, 7*(4), 485–496.

Allinder, R. M. (1994). The relationship between efficacy and the instructional practices of special education teachers and consultants. *Teacher Education and Special Education, 17*(2), 86–95.

Ambady, N., Bernieri, F. J., & Richeson, J. A. (2000). Toward a histology of social behavior: Judgmental accuracy from thin slices of the behavioral stream. In M. P. Zanna (Ed.), *Advances in experimental social psychology* (vol. 32, pp. 201–271). San Diego, CA: Academic Press.

Ambady, N., & Gray, H. M. (2002). On being sad and mistaken: Mood effects on the accuracy of thin-slice judgments. *Journal of Personality & Social Psychology, 8* 3(4), 947–961.

Ambady, N., & Rosenthal, R. (1992). Half a minute: Predicting teacher evaluations from thin slices of nonverbal behavior and physical attractiveness. *Journal of Personality and Social Psychology, 64,* 431–441.

American Association for the Advancement of Science. (1993). *Benchmarks for science literacy: Project 2061.* New York: Oxford University Press.

American Federation of Teachers. (2001). *Making standards matter.* Washington, DC: Author.

American Federation of Teachers. (2008). *Survey and analysis of teacher salary trends, 2007.* Retrieved December 28, 2009 from http://www.aft.org/salary/2007/download/AFT2007SalarySurvey.pdf

Amrein-Beardsley, A. (2008). Methodological concerns about the education value-added assessment system. *Educational Researcher, 37*(2), 65–75.

Andrew, M. D., Cobb, C. D., & Giampietro, P. J. (2005). Verbal ability and teacher effectiveness. *Journal of Teacher Education, 56*(4), 343–354. DOI: 10.1177/0022487105279928

Armor, D., Conry-Oseguera, P., Cox, M., King, N., McDonnell, L., Pascal, A., Pauly, E., & Zellman, G. (1976). *Analysis of the school preferred reading program in selected Los Angeles minority schools.* (R-2007-LAUSD). Santa Monica, CA: RAND.

Ashton, P. T., & Webb, R. B. (1986). *Making a difference: Teachers' sense of efficacy and student achievement.* New York: Longman.

Ashton, P., Webb, R., & Doda, N. (1983). *A study of teachers' sense of efficacy.* (Final Report, National Institute of Education Contract No. 400-79-0075.) Gainesville: University of Florida. (ERIC Document ED 231 834).

Aslam, M., & Kingdon, G. (2007). *What can Teachers do to Raise Pupil Achievement?* The Centre for the Study of African Economies Working Paper Series. CSAE Paper 273: Berkeley Electronic Press. Retrieved August 14, 2010, from http://www.bepress.com/cgi/viewcontent. cgi?article = 1273&context = csae

Bacolod, M. P. (2007). Do alternative opportunities matter? The role of female labor markets in the decline of teacher quality. *The Review of Economics and Statistics, 89*(4), 737–751.

Baker, E. L., Barton, P. E., Darling-Hammond, L., Haertel, E., Ladd, H. F., Linn, R. L., et al. (2010). *Problems with the use of student test scores to evaluate teachers.* Washington, DC: Economic Policy Institute.

Ballou, D. (2003). Certifying accomplished teachers: A critical look at the National Board for Professional Teaching Standards. *Peabody Journal of Education, 78*(4), 201–219.

Ballou, D. (2009). Test scaling and value-added measurement. *Education Finance and Policy, 4*(4), 351–383.

Ballou, D., & Podgursky, M. (1993). Teachers attitudes toward merit pay: Examining conventional wisdom. *Industrial and Labor Relations Review, 47*(1), 50–61.

Ballou, D., Sanders, W., & Wright, P. (2004). Controlling for student background in value-added assessment of teachers. *Journal of Educational and Behavioral Statistics, 29*(1), 37–65.

Bandura, A. (1982). Self-efficacy mechanism in human agency. *American Psychologist, 37*(2), 122–147.

Baron, R., Tom, D. Y. H., & Cooper, H. M. (1985). Social class, race and teacher expectations. In J. B. Dusek (Ed.), *Teacher expectancies* (pp. 251–269). Hillsdale, NJ: Lawrence Erlbaum.

Barron's Educational Series. (2009). *Profiles of American colleges* (28th ed.). Hauppauge, NY: Author.

Beard, R. (2000). Research and the national literacy strategy. *Oxford Review of Education 26*(3–4), 421–436.

Bee, M., & Dolton, P. (1995). The remuneration of school teachers: Time series and cross-section evidence. *Manchester School of Economic and Social Studies, 63*(1), 1–22.

Benjamin, D. J., & Shapiro, J. M. (2009). Thin-slice forecasts of gubernatorial elections. *The Review of Economics and Statistics, 91*(3), 523–536.

Berliner, D. (2005). The near impossibility of testing for teacher quality. *Journal of Teacher Education, 56*(3), 205–213.

Berman, P., & McLaughlin, M. W. (1977). *Federal programs supporting educational change: Vol. 7. Factors affecting implementation and continuation.* (R-1589/5-HEW). Santa Monica, CA: RAND.

Betts, J. R., Zau, A. C., & Rice, L. A. (2003). *Determinants of student achievement: New evidence from San Diego.* San Francisco: Public Policy Institute of California. Retrieved February 10, 2010, from http://epsl.asu.edu/epru/articles/EPRU-0309-39-OWI.pdf

Blanton, L., Sindelar, P. T., Correa, V., Hardman, M., McDonnell, J., & Kuhel, K. (2003). *Conceptions of beginning teacher quality: Models of conducting research. (COPSSE Document*

Number RS-6). Gainesville: University of Florida, Center on Personnel Studies in Special Education.

Blau, P., & Duncan, O. D. (1967). *The American occupational structure*. New York: Wiley.

Bommer, W. H., Johnson, J. L., Rich, G. A., Podsakoff, P. M., & MacKenzie, S. B. (1995). On the interchangeability of objective and subjective measures of employee performance: A meta-analysis. *Personnel Psychology, 48*(3),587–605.

Borko, H., Stecher, B. M., Alonzo, A. C., Moncure, S., & McClam, S. (2005). Artifact packages for characterizing classroom practice: A pilot study. *Educational Assessment, 10*(2), 73–104.

Borko, H., Stecher, B. M., Martinez, F., Kuffner, K. L., Barnes, D., Arnold, S. C., et al. (2006). *Using classroom artifacts to measure instructional practice in middle school science: A two-state field test*. Los Angeles: National Center for Research on Evaluation, Standards, and Student Testing.

Borko, H., Stecher, B. M., & Kuffner, K. (2007). *Using artifacts to characterize reform-oriented instruction: The scoop notebook and rating guide* (CSE Technical Report No. 207). Los Angeles: Center for Evaluation, Standards and Student Testing (CRESST), University of California at Los Angeles. Retrieved September 17, 2010, from http://www.cse.ucla.edu/products/reports/r707.pdfBorman, G. D., & Kimball, S. M. (2005). Teacher quality and educational equality: Do teachers with higher standards-based evaluation ratings close student achievement gaps? *The Elementary School Journal, 106*(1), 3–20.

Boyd, D., Grossman, P., Lankford, H., Loeb, S., & Wyckoff, J. (2006). How changes in entry requirements alter the teacher workforce and affect student achievement. *Education Finance and Policy, 1*(2), 176–216.

Brandt, C., Mathers, C., Oliva, M., Brown-Sims, M., & Hess, J. (2007). *Examining district guidance to schools on teacher evaluation policies in the Midwest region* (Issues & Answers Report, REL 2007–No. 030). Washington, DC: U.S. Department of Education, Institute of Education Sciences, National Center for Education Evaluation and Regional Assistance, Regional Educational Laboratory Midwest. Retrieved October 12, 2009, from http://ies.ed.gov/ncee/edlabs

Braun, C. (1976). Teacher expectation: Sociopsychological dynamics. *Review of Educational Research, 46*(2), 185–213.

Braun, H., Chudowsky, N., & Koenig, J. (Eds.). (2010). *Getting value out of value-added: Report of a workshop*. Committee on Value-Added Methodology for Instructional Improvement, Program Evaluation, and Accountability; National Research Council. Retrieved September 23, 2010, from http://www.nap.edu/catalog/12820.html

Brophy, J. (1986). Teacher influences on student achievement. *American Psychologist, 41*(10), 1069–1077.

Brophy, J., & Evertson, C. (1976). *Learning from teaching: A developmental perspective*. Boston: Allyn and Bacon.

Brophy, J., & Good, T. (1974). *Teacher-student relationships: Causes and consequences*. New York: Holt.

Brophy, J., & Good, T. (1986). Teacher behavior and student achievement. In M. C. Witrock (Ed.), *Handbook of research and teaching* (3rd ed.). New York: Macmillan.

Brown, N., Morehead, P., & Smith, J. B. (2008). . . . But I love children: Changing elementary teacher candidates' conceptions of the qualities of effective teachers. *Teacher Education Quarterly, 35*(1), 169–183.

Burstein, L., McDonnell, L. M., Van Winkle, J., Ormseth, T., Mirocha, J., & Guitton, G. (1995). *Validating national curriculum indicators.* Santa Monica, CA: RAND.

California Department of Education. (1985). *Mathematics framework for California public schools: Kindergarten through grade twelve.* Sacramento, CA: Author.

Camburn, E., & Barnes, C. A. (2004). Assessing the validity of a language arts instruction log through triangulation. *Elementary School Journal, 105*(1), 49–74.

Camburn, E., & Han, S. W. (2006*). Factors affecting the validity of teachers' reports of instructional practice on annual surveys* (Working paper of the Consortium for Policy Research in Education). Madison: Wisconsin Center for Education Research.

Campbell, R. J., Kyriakides, L., Muijs, R. D., & Robinson, W. (2003). Differential teacher effectiveness: Towards a model for research and teacher appraisal. *Oxford Review of Education, 29*(3), 347–362.

Campbell, R. J., Kyriakides, L., Muijs, D., & Robinson, W. (2004). *Assessing teacher effectiveness: Developing a differentiated model.* New York: Routledge Falmer.

Carlgren, I. (1999). Professionalism and teachers as designers. *Journal of Curriculum Studies, 31*(1), 43–56.

Carnegie Task Force on Teaching, Carnegie Corporation. (1986). *A nation prepared: Teachers for the 21st century.* New York: Author.

Carr, M. (2006). *The determinants of student achievement in Ohio's public schools: Kindergarten through grade twelve.* Columbus, OH: Buckeye Institute for Public Policy Solutions.

Cavalluzzo, L. C. (2004). *Is National Board Certification an effective signal of teacher quality?* (Report No. IPR 11204). Alexandria, VA: The CNA Corporation.

Chaiken, S., & Trope, Y. (Eds.). (1999). *Dual-process theories in social psychology.* New York: Guilford Press.

Chait, R. (2009). *From qualifications to results: Promoting teacher effectiveness through federal policy.* Washington DC: Center for American Progress. Retrieved February 12, 2009, from http://www.guilford.k12.nc.us/whatmatters/pdf/Center%20for%20American%20Progress.pdf

Christensen-Szalanski, J. J. (1991). The hindsight bias: A meta-analysis. *Organizational Behavior and Human Decision Processes, 48*(1), 147–168.

Clare, L., & Aschbacher, P. (2001). Exploring the technical quality of using assignments and student work as indicators of classroom practice, *Educational Assessment, 7*(1), 39–59.

Clewell, B. C., & Villegas, A. M. (1998). Diversifying the teaching force to improve urban schools: Meeting the challenge—Introduction. *Education and Urban Society, 31*(1), 3–17.

Clotfelter, C., Ladd, H., & Vigdor, J. (2006). *Teacher-student matching and the assessment of teacher effectiveness.* (NBER Working Paper No. 11936). Cambridge, MA: National Bureau of Economic Research.

Clotfelter, C., Ladd, H., & Vigdor, J. (2007a). *How and why do teacher credentials matter for student achievement?* (NBER Working Paper No. 12828). Cambridge, MA: National Bureau of Economic Research.

Clotfelter, C., Ladd, H., & Vigdor, J. (2007b). Teacher credentials and student achievement: Longitudinal analysis with student fixed effects. *Economics of Education Review, 26*(6), 673–682.

Clotfelter, C., Ladd, H., & Vigdor, J. (2007c). *Teacher credentials and student achievement in high school: A cross-subject analysis with student fixed effects.* (NBER Working Paper No. 13617.) Cambridge, MA: National Bureau of Economic Research.

Cohen, D. K. (2010). Teacher quality: An American educational dilemma. In M. Kennedy (Ed.), *Teacher assessment and the quest for teacher quality: A handbook.* San Francisco, CA: Jossey-Bass.

Cohen, D. K., & Hill, H. C. (2000). Instructional policy and classroom performance: The mathematics reform in California. *Teachers College Record, 102*(2), 294–343.

Coleman, J. S., Campbell, E. Q., Hobson, C. J., McPartland, J., Mood, A. M., Weinfeld, F. D., & York, R. (1966). *Equality of educational opportunity.* Washington, DC: National Center for Educational Statistics.

Combs, A. W., Blume, R. A., Newman, A. J., & Wass, H. L. (1974). *The professional education of teachers: A humanistic approach to teacher preparation.* Boston: Allyn and Bacon.

Constantine, J., Player, D., Silva, T., Hallgren, K., Grider, M., & Deke, J. (2009, February). *An evaluation of teachers trained through different routes to certification: Final report.* Princeton, NJ: Mathematica Policy Research Inc. Retrieved March 4, 2010, from http://www.mathematica-mpr.com/publications/PDFs/Education/ teacherstrained09.pdf

Cooper, H. (1979). Pygmalion grows up: A model for teacher expectation communication and performance influence. *Review of Educational Research, 49*(3), 389–410.

Corcoran, S. P., Evans, W. N., & Schwab, R. M. (2004). Women, the labor market, and the declining relative quality of teachers. *Journal of Policy Analysis and Management, 23*(3), 449–470.

Corcoran, S. P., & Jennings, J. L. (2009). Review of *"An evaluation of teachers trained through different routes to certification: Final report."* Boulder and Tempe: Education and the Public Interest Center and Education Policy Research Unit. Retrieved March 4, 2010, from http:// epicpolicy.org/thinktank/review-evaluation-of-teachers

Correnti, R. (2007). An empirical investigation of professional development effects on literacy instruction using daily logs. *Educational Evaluation and Policy Analysis, 29*(4), 239–261.

Correnti, R., & Rowan, B. (2007). Opening up the black box: Literacy instruction in schools participating in three comprehensive school reform programs. *American Educational Research Journal, 44*(2), 298–338.

Counts, G. S. (1925). The social status of occupations: A problem in vocational guidance. *The School Review, 33*(1), 16–27.

Cronbach, L. J. (1971). Test validation. In R. L. Thorndike (Ed.), *Educational measurement* (2nd ed., pp. 443–507). Washington, DC: American Council on Education.

Cronbach, L. J. (1988). Five perspectives on validity argument. In H. Wainer & H. Braun (Eds.), *Test validity* (pp. 3–17). Hillsdale, NJ: Lawrence Erlbaum.

Danielson, C. (2007). *Enhancing professional practice: A framework for teaching.* Alexandria, VA: Association for Supervision and Curriculum Development.

Davis, F. D., Lohse, G. L., & Kottemann, J. E. (1994). Harmful effects of seemingly helpful information on forecasts of stock earnings. *Journal of Economic Psychology, 15*(2), 253–267.

Darling-Hammond, L. (1990). Teaching and knowledge: Policy issues posed by alternative certification for teachers. *Peabody Journal of Education, 67*(3), 123–154.

Darling-Hammond, L. (1996). What matters most: A competent teacher for every child. *Phi Delta Kappan, 78*(3), 193–201.

Darling-Hammond, L. (1997). *The right to learn: A blueprint for creating schools that work.* San Francisco, CA: Jossey-Bass.

Darling-Hammond, L. (2001). The research and rhetoric on teacher certification: A response to "Teacher Certification Reconsidered." Retrieved March 27, /2010, from http://www.nctaf. org/documents/abell_response.pdf

Darling-Hammond, L. (2002). The research and rhetoric on teacher certification: A response to "Teacher Certification Reconsidered." *Educational Policy Analysis Archives, 10*(36). Retrieved March 5, /2010, from http://epaa.asu.edu/epaa/v10n36.html

Darling-Hammond, L., Berry, B., & Thoreson, A. (2001). Does teacher certification matter? Evaluating the evidence. *Educational Evaluation and Policy Analysis, 23*(1), 57–77.

Darling-Hammond, L., Holtzman, D. J., Gatlin, S. J., & Heilig, J. V. (2005). Does teacher preparation matter? Evidence about teacher certification, Teach for America, and teacher effectiveness. *Education Policy Analysis Archives, 13*(42). Retrieved February 11, from http://epaa. asu.edu/epaa/v13n42/

Darling-Hammond, L., & Youngs, P. (2002). Defining "highly-qualified teachers." What does "scientifically-based research" actually tell us? *Educational Researcher, 31*(9), 13–25.

Decker, P. T., Mayer, D. P., & Glazerman, S. (2004). *The Effects of Teach For America on Students: Findings from a National Evaluation.* Princeton, NJ: Mathematica Policy Research, Inc.

Decker, P. T., Mayer, D. P., & Glazerman, S. (2004). *The effects of Teach For America on students: Finding from a national evaluation.* Princeton, NJ: Mathematica Policy Associates. Retrieved March 4, /2010, from http://www.mathematica-mpr.com/publications/pdfs/teach.pdf

Dee, T. S. (2004). Teachers, race and student achievement in a randomized experiment. *Review of Economics and Statistics, 86*(1), 195–210.

Dee, T. S. (2005). A teacher like me: Does race, ethnicity, or gender matter? *The American Economic Review, 95*(2), 158–165.

Dillon, S. (2010, August 31). Formula to grade teachers' skill gains acceptance, and critics. *Los Angeles Times* [on line edition], retrieved September 4, 2010 from http://www.nytimes. com/2010/09/01/education/01teacher.html?_r=1&pagewanted%20=%201&_r%20=%20 1&hp

Downey, C. J., Steffy, B. E., English, F. W., Frase, L. E., & Poston, W. K., Jr. (2004). *The three-minute classroom walk-through: Changing school supervisory practice one teacher at a time.* Thousand Oaks, CA: Corwin Press.

Dublin, T. (1983). Women's work and the family economy: Textiles and palm leaf hatmaking in New England, 1830–1850. *Tocqueville Review, 5*(2), 297–316.

Dusek, J. (1975). Do teachers bias children's learning? *Review of Educational Research, 45*(4), 661–684.

Ehrenberg, R., & Brewer, D. (1994). Do school and teacher characteristics matter? Evidence from *high school and beyond. Economics of Education Review, 13*(1), 1–17.

Ehrenberg, R. G., & Brewer, D. J. (1995). Did teachers' verbal ability and race matter in the 1960s? *Coleman* revisited. *Economics of Education Review, 14*(1), 1–21.

Ehrenberg, R. G., Goldhaber, D. D., & Brewer, D. J. (1995). Do teachers' race, gender, and ethnicity matter? Evidence from the National Educational Longitudinal Study of 1988 *Industrial and Labor Relations Review, 48*(3), 547–561.

Eide, E., Goldhaber, D., & Brewer, D. (2004). The teacher labour market and teacher quality. *Oxford Review of Economic Policy, 20*(2), 230–244.

Elashoff, J. D., & Snow, R. E. (1971). *Pygmalion reconsidered.* Worthington, OH: Charles A. Jones.

Epstein, S. (1994). Integration of the cognitive and psychodynamic unconscious. *American Psychologist, 49*(8), 709–724.

Etzioni, A. (Ed.). (1969). *The semi-professions and their organization: Teachers, nurses, social workers.* New York, London: The Free Press.

Falch, J., Song, J., & Smith, D. (2010, August 14). Grading the teachers: Who's teaching L.A.'s kids? *Los Angeles Times* [on line edition], retrieved August 14, 2010, from http://www.latimes.com/news/local/la-me-teachers-value-20100815,0,258862,full.story.

Fenstermacher, G. (1990). The place of alternative certification in the education of teachers. *Peabody Journal of Education, 67*(3), 155–185.

Fenstermacher, G. D., & Richardson, V. (2005). On making determinations of quality in teaching. *Teachers College Record, 107*(1), 186–213.

Ferguson, R. F. (1991). Paying for public education: New evidence on how and why money matters. *Harvard Journal on Legislation, 28,* 465–498.

Ferguson, R. F. (2003). Teachers' perceptions and expectations and the black-white test score gap. *Urban Education, 38* (4), 460–507.

Ferguson, R. F., & Brown, J. (2000). Certification test scores, teacher quality, and student achievement. In D. Grissmer & J. M. Ross (Eds.), *Analytic issues in the assessment of student achievement* (pp. 133–156). Washington, DC: National Center for Education Statistics.

Fetler, M. (1997). Staffing up and dropping out: Unintended consequences of high demand for teachers. *Education Policy Analysis Archives, 5*(16), retrieved February 4, 2010 from http://olam.ed.asu.edu/epaa/v5n16html.

Finn, J. (1972). Expectations and the educational environment. *Review of Educational Research, 42*(3), 387–410.

Fischhoff, B. (2001). Learning from experience: Coping with hindsight bias and ambiguity. In J. S. Armstrong (Ed.), *Principles of Forecasting* (pp. 484–494). Norwell, MA: Kluwer Academic Press.

Follman, J. (1992). Secondary school students' ratings of teacher effectiveness. *The High School Journal, 75*(3), 168–178.

Follman, J. (1995). Elementary public school pupil rating of teacher effectiveness. *Child Study Journal, 25*(1), 57–78.

Frederick, S. (2005). Cognitive reflection and decision making. *Journal of Economic Perspectives, 19*(4), 25–42.

Frome, P., Lasater, B., & Cooney, S. (2005). *Well qualified teachers and high quality teaching: Are they the same?* Research Brief. Atlanta, GA: Southern Regional Education Board. Retrieved

October 10, 2009 from http://publications.sreb.org/2005/05V06_Research_Brief_high-quality_teaching.pdf.

Gallagher, H. A. (2004). Vaughn Elementary's innovative teacher evaluation system: Are teacher evaluation scores related to growth in student achievement? *Peabody Journal of Education, 79*(4), 79–107.

Getzels, J. W., & Jackson, P. W. (1963). The teacher's personality. In N. L. Gage (Ed.), *Handbook of research on teaching*, (pp. 506–582). Chicago: Rand McNally.

Glazerman, S., Goldhaber, D., Loeb, S., Staiger, D. O., & Whitehurst, G. J. (2010). *America's Teacher Corps.* Washington, DC: The Brookings Institution, Brown Center on Education Policy.

Goddard, R. D., Hoy, W. K., & Hoy, A. W. (2000). Collective teacher efficacy: Its meaning, measure, and impact on student achievement. *American Educational Research Journal, 37*(2), 479–507.

Goe, L. (2007). *The link between teacher quality and student outcomes: A research synthesis.* Washington, DC: NCCTQ.

Goldhaber, D. (2002). Teacher quality and teacher pay structure: What do we know, and what are the options? *Georgetown Public Policy Review, 7*(2), 81–94.

Goldhaber, D., & Anthony, E. (2007). Can teacher quality be effectively assessed? National Board Certification as a signal of effective teaching. *The Review of Economics and Statistics, 89*(1), 134–150.

Goldhaber, D. D., & Brewer, D. J. (1997). Evaluating the effect of teacher degree level on educational performance. In W. J. Fowler (Ed.), *Developments in school finance, 1996* (pp. 197–210). Washington, DC: National Center for Education Statistics, U.S. Department of Education.

Goldhaber, D. D., & Brewer, D. J. (2000). Does teacher certification matter? High school teacher certification status and student achievement. *Educational Evaluation and Policy Analysis, 22*(2), 129–145.

Goldhaber, D. D., & Hansen, M. (2010). *Assessing the potential of using value-added estimates of teacher job performance for making tenure decisions.* Working Paper 31. Washington, DC: CALDER, The Urban Institute. Retrieved March 26, 2010, from http://www.urban.org/publications/1001369.html

Good, T. (1981). A decade of research on teacher expectations. *Educational Leadership, 38*(5), 415–423.

Good, T. (1983). Classroom research: A decade of progress. *Educational Psychologist, 18*(3), 127–144.

Graham, P. A. (1987). Black teachers: A drastically scarce resource. *Phi Delta Kappan, 68*(8), 598–605.

Grossman, P., Loeb, S., Cohen, J., Hammerness, K., Wyckoff, J., Boyd, D., et al. (2010). *Measure for measure: The relationship between measures of instructional practice in middle school English language arts and teachers' value-added scores.* Working Paper 45. Washington, DC: CALDER, The Urban Institute.

Hamre, B. K., & Pianta, R. C. (2005). Can instructional and emotional support in the first-grade classroom make a difference for children at risk of school failure? *Child Development, 76*(5), 949–967.

Hanushek, E. A. (1992). The trade-off between child quantity and quality. *Journal of Political Economy, 100*(1), 85–117.

Hanushek, E. A. (1971). Teacher characteristics and gains in student achievement: Estimation using micro data. *American Economic Review, 60*(2), 280–288.

Hanushek, E. A. (1996). A more complete picture of school resource policies. *Review of Educational Research, 66*(3), 397–409.

Hanushek, E. A. (1997). Assessing the effects of school resources on student performance: An update. *Educational Evaluation and Policy Analysis, 19*(2), 141–164.

Hanushek, E. A. (2003). The failure of input-based schooling policies. *Economic Journal, 113*(485), F64–F98.

Hanuskek, E. A. (2010). *The economic value of high teacher quality.* NBER Working Paper 16606. Cambridge, MA: National Bureau of Economic Research.

Hanushek, E. A., Kain, J. F., O'Brien, D. M., & Rivkin, S. G. (2005). *The market for teacher quality.* (Working Paper No. 11154). Cambridge, MA: National Bureau for Economic Research.

Hanushek, E. A., Kain, J. F., Rivkin, S. G. (2004). Why public schools lose teachers. *Journal of Human Resources, 39*(2), 326–354.

Hanushek, E. A., & Rivkin, S. G. (2006). Teacher quality. In E. A. Hanushek & F. Welch, (Eds.), *Handbook of the Economics of Education, Volume 2* (pp. 1052–1075). Amsterdam, NL: North-Holland.

Hanushek, E. A., Rivkin, S. G., Rothstein, R., & Podgursky, M. (2004). How to improve the supply of high-quality teachers. In D. Ravitch (Ed.), *Brookings Papers on Education Policy* (pp. 7–44). Washington, DC: Brookings Institution Press.

Harbison, R. W., & Hanushek, E. A. (1992). *Educational performance of the poor: Lessons from rural northeast Brazil.* New York: Oxford University Press.

Hargreaves, A. (2000). Four ages of professionalism and professional learning. *Teachers and Teaching: Theory and Practice, 6*(2), 151–182.

Hargreaves, A. and Goodson, I. (1996) Teachers professional lives: aspirations and actualities, in: I. Goodson and A, Hargreaves (Eds.) *Teachers' Professional LivesI* (pp. 1–27). London: Falmer Press.

Hargreaves, L., Cunningham, M., Everton, T., Hansen, A., Hopper, B., McIntyre, D., et al. (2006). *The status of teachers and the teaching profession: Views from inside and outside the profession.* Cambridge: Chancellor, Masters, and Scholars of the University of Cambridge.

Harris, D. N. (2009). Would accountability based on teacher value added be smart policy? An examination of the statistical properties and policy alternatives. *Education Finance and Policy, 4*(4), 319–350.

Harris, D. N., & Sass, T. R. (2007). *What makes a good teacher and who can tell?* Paper presented at the summer workshop of the National Bureau of Economic Research, Cambridge, MA.

Harris, D. N., & Sass, T. (2008). *Teacher training, teacher quality and student achievement.* Tallahassee, FL: Florida State University, unpublished manuscript. Retrieved October 4, 2009, from http://mailer.fsu.edu/~tsass/Papers/IES%20Harris%20Sass%20Teacher%20Training%2031.pdf

Harris, D. N., & Sass, T. (2009). The effects of NBPTS-certified teachers on student achievement. *Journal of Policy Analysis and Management, 28*(1), 55–80.

Hawk, P., Coble, C. R., & Swanson, M. (1985). Certification: It does matter. *Journal of Teacher Education, 36*(3), 13–15.

Hawkins, S. A., & Hastie, R. (1990). Hindsight: Biased judgments of past events after the outcomes are known. *Psychological Bulletin, 107*(3), 311–327.

Heneman, R. L. (1986). The relationship between supervisory ratings and results-oriented measures performance: A meta-analysis. *Personnel Psychology, 39*(4), 811–826.

Heneman, H. G., Milanowski, A., Kimball, S. M., & Odden, A. (2006). *Standards-based teacher evaluation as a foundation for knowledge- and skill-based pay.* CPRE Policy Brief No. RB-45. Philadelphia, PA: Consortium for Policy Research in Education. Retrieved 7/14/2010, from http://www.cpre.org/images/stories/cpre_pdfs/RB45.pdf

Hill, H. C., Blunk, M. L., Charalambous, C. Y., Lewis, J. M., Phelps, G. C., Sleep, L., et al. (2008). Mathematical knowledge for teaching and the mathematical quality of instruction: An exploratory study. *Cognition And Instruction, 26*(4), 430–511.

Hill, H. C., Rowan, B., & Ball, D. L. (2005). Effects of teachers' mathematical knowledge for teaching on student achievement. *American Educational Research Journal, 42*(2), 371–406.

Hill, H. C., Umland, K., & Kapitula, L. R. (2010). *Validating value-added scores: An instructional analysis.* Paper presented at the annual meeting of the American Educational Research Association, Denver, Co., May 3.

Hodge, R. W., Siegel, P. M., & Rossi, P. H. (1964). Occupational prestige in the United States, 1925–63. *American Journal of Sociology, 70*(3), 286–302.

Hodge, R. W., Treiman, D., & Rossi, P. H. (1966). A comparative study of occupational prestige. In R. Bendix & S. M. Lipset (Eds.), *Class, Status, and Power* (2nd ed., pp. 309–321). New York: Free Press.

Hofer, M. A. (1994, December 26). Behind the curve. *The New York Times,* pp. A39.

Holtzapple, E. (2003). Criterion-related validity evidence for a standards-based teacher evaluation system. *Journal of Personnel Evaluation in Education, 17*(3), 207–219.

Howes, C., Burchinal, M., Pianta, R. C., Bryant, D., Early, D., Clifford, R., et al. (2008). Ready to learn? Children's pre-academic achievement in pre-kindergarten programs. *Early Childhood Research Quarterly, 23*(1), 27–50.

Hoyle, E. (2008). Changing conceptions of teaching as a profession: Personal reflections. In D. Johnson & R. Maclean (Eds.), *Teaching: Professionalization, Development and Leadership* (pp. 285–304). Dordrecht, The Netherlands: Springer.

Hyland, T. (1996). Professionalism, ethics and work-based learning. *British Journal of Educational Studies, 44*(2), 168–180.

Ingersoll, R. M., & Merrill, L. (2010). Who's teaching our children? *Educational Leadership, 67*(8), 14–20.

Ingersoll, R. M., & Perda, D. (2008). The status of teaching as a profession. In J. Ballantine & J. Spade (Eds.), *Schools and Society: a Sociological Approach to Education* (pp. 106–118), Los Angeles: Pine Forge Press.

Jacob, B. A., & Lefgren, L. (2008). Can principals identify effective teachers? Evidence on subjective performance evaluation in education. *Journal of Labor Economics, 26*(1), 101–136.

James, W. (1950). *The principles of psychology*. New York: Dover. (Originally published 1890)

Jepsen, C., & Rivkin, S. G. (2002). *What is the trade-off between smaller classes and teacher quality?* Working Paper 9205. Cambridge, MA: National Bureau of Economic Research. Retrieved October 4, 2009, from http://www.aiecon.org/advanced/suggestedreadings/PDF/sug264.pdf

Johnson-Laird, P. N. (1983). *Mental models*. Cambridge, MA: Harvard University Press.

Jones, E. E. (1986). Interpreting interpersonal behavior: The effects of expectancies. *Science, 234*(4772), 41–46.

Jones, R., & Swanson, E. (2009). Understanding elementary teachers' use of science teaching time: Lessons from the Big Sky Science Partnership. *The Journal of Mathematics and Science: Collaborative Explorations, 11*, 163–192.

Jussim, L., Eccles, J., & Madon, S. J. (1996). Social perception, social stereotypes, and teacher expectations: Accuracy and the quest for the powerful self-fulfilling prophecy. *Advances in experimental social psychology, 29*(2), 281–388.

Jussim, L., & Harber, K. D. (2005). Teacher expectations and self-fulfilling prophecies: Knowns and unknowns, resolved and unresolved controversies. *Personality and Social Psychology Review, 9*(2), 131–155.

Kahneman, D. (2002). *Maps of bounded rationality: A perspective on intuitive judgment and choice*. Nobel Prize Lecture, December 8. Retrieved February 29, 2008, from http://nobelprize.org/nobel_prizes/economics/laureates/2002/kahnemann-lecture.pdf

Kahneman, D., & Frederick, S. (2002). Representativeness revisited: Attribute substitution in intuitive judgment. In T. Gilovich, D. Griffin & D. Kahneman (Eds.), *Heuristics and Biases* (pp. 49–81). New York: Cambridge University Press.

Kahneman, D., & Frederick, S. (2005). A model of heuristic judgment. In K. J. Holyoak & R. G. Morrison (Eds.), *The Cambridge handbook of thinking and reasoning* (pp. 267–293). New York: Cambridge University Press.

Kane, T. J., Rockoff, J. E., & Staiger, D. O. (2008). What does certification tell us about teacher effectiveness? Evidence from New York City. *Economics of Education Review, 27*(6), 615–631.

Kane, M. (2006). Validation. In R. Brennan (Ed.), *Educational measurement* (4th ed., pp. 17–64). Westport, CT: American Council on Education and Praeger.

Kane, T. J., Taylor, E. S., Tyler, J. H., & Wooten, A. L. (2010). *Identifying effective classroom practices using student achievement data*. NBER Working Paper 15803. Cambridge, MA: National Bureau of Economic Research.

Kannapel, P. J., & Clements, S. K. (with Taylor, D., & Hibpshman, T.). (2005). *Inside the black box of high-performing, high-poverty schools*. Lexington, KY: Prichard Committee for Academic Excellence. Retrieved March 11, 2010, from http://inpathways.net/FordReportJE.pdf

Kimball, S. M., White, B., Milanowski, A. T., & Borman, G. (2004). Examining the relationship between teacher evaluation and student assessment results in Washoe County. *Peabody Journal of Education, 79*(4), 54–78.

Koedel, C., & Betts, J. (2007). *Re-examining the role of teacher quality in the educational production function*. Working paper No. 0708, University of Missouri. Retrieved August 16, 2010, from http://client.norc.org/jole/SOLEweb/Koedel_Betts.pdf

Korthagen, F. A. J. (2004). In search of the essence of a good teacher: Towards a more holistic approach in teacher education. *Teaching and Teacher Education, 20*(1), 77–97.

Kunda, Z. (1990). The case for motivated reasoning. *Psychological Bulletin, 108*(3), 480–498.

Kupermintz, H. (2003). Teacher effects and teacher effectiveness: A validity investigation of the Tennessee Value Added Assessment System. *Educational Evaluation and Policy Analysis, 25*(3), 287–298.

Laczko-Kerr, I., & Berliner, D. (2002). The effectiveness of Teach for America and other under-certified teachers on student academic achievement: A case of harmful public policy. *Educational Policy Analysis Archives, 10*(37). Retrieved March 4, 2010, from http://epaa.asu.edu/epaa/v10n37/

Lakdawalla, D. (2001). The declining quality of teachers. *NBER Working Paper 8263*, Cambridge, MA: National Bureau of Economic Research. Retrieved November 12, 2009, from http://www.nber.org/papers/w8263

Lakdawalla, D. (2006). The economics of teacher quality. *Journal of Law and Economics, 49*(1), 285–329.

Lasley, T. J. (1980). Preservice teacher beliefs about teaching. *Journal of Teacher Education, 31*(4), 38–41.

Learning Mathematics for Teaching. (2006). *A coding rubric for measuring the quality of mathematics in instruction* (Technical Report LMT1.06). Ann Arbor, MI: University of Michigan, School of Education.

LoCasale-Crouch, J., Konold, T., Pianta, R. C., Howes, C., Burchinal, M., Bryant, D., et al. (2007). Observed classroom quality profiles in state-funded pre-kindergarten programs and associations with teacher, program, and classroom characteristics. *Early Childhood Research Quarterly, 22*(1), 3–17.

Lockwood, J. R., McCaffrey, D., Hamilton, L., Stecher, B., Le, V-N., & Martinez, J. F. (2007). The sensitivity of value-added teacher effect estimates to different mathematics achievement measures. *Journal of Educational Measurement 44*(1), 47–67.

Machin, S., & McNally, S. (2008). The literacy hour. *Journal of Public Economics, 92*(5–6),1441–1462.

Mack, A., & Rock, I. (1998). *Inattentional blindness.* Cambridge, MA: MIT Press.

Madon, S. J., Jussim, L., & Eccles, J. (1997). In search of the powerful self-fulfilling prophecy. *Journal of Personality and Social Psychology 72*(4), 791–809.

Manski, C. F. (1985). Academic ability, earnings, and the decision to become a teacher. Evidence from the National Longitudinal Study of the High School Class of 1972. *NBER Working Paper 1539.* Cambridge, MA: National Bureau of Economic Research.

Marcoulides, G. A., Heck, R. H., & Papanastasiou, C. (2005). Student perceptions of school culture and achievement: Testing the invariance of a model. *International Journal of Educational Management, 19*(2), 140–152.

Mashburn, A. J., Pianta, R. C., Hamre, B. K., Downer, J. T., Barbarin, O. A., Bryant, D., et al. (2008). Measures of classroom quality in prekindergarten and children's development of academic, language, and social skills. *Child Development, 79*(3), 732–749.

Maslow, A. H. (1968). *Toward a psychology of being* (2nd ed.). Princeton, NJ: Van Nostrand.

Matsumura, L. C., Slater, S. C., Junker, B., Peterson, M., Boston, M., Steele, M., et al. (2006). *Measuring reading comprehension and mathematics instruction in urban middle schools: A pilot study of the instructional quality assessment* (CSE Technical Report 681). Los Angeles: National Center for Research on Evaluation, Standards, and Student Testing.

Mayer, D. P. (1999). Measuring instructional practice: Can policymakers trust survey data? *Educational Evaluation and Policy Analysis, 21*(1), 29–45.

McCaffrey, D. F., Han, B., & Lockwood, J. R. (2008). *From data to bonuses: A case study of the issues related to awarding teachers pay on the basis of their students' progress.* Working paper No. 2008-4, National Center on Performance Incentives, Vanderbilt University. Retrieved 9/25/2010, from http://www.performanceincentives.org/data/files/news/ReportsNews/McCaffrey_Feb_08.pdf

McCaffrey D. F., Han, B., & Lockwood J. R. (2009). Turning student test scores into teacher compensation systems. In M. G. Springer (Ed.), *Performance incentives: Their growing impact on American K–12 education.* Washington, DC: The Brookings Institute.

McCaffrey, D. F., Lockwood, J. R., Koretz, D. M., Louis, T. A., & Hamilton, L. S. (2004). Models for value-added modeling of teacher effects. *Journal of Educational and Behavioral Statistics, 29*(1), 67–101.

McCaffrey, D. F., Sass, T. R., Lockwood, J. R., & Mihaly, K. (2009). The intertemporal variability of teacher effect estimates. *Education Finance and Policy, 4*(4), 572–606.

McColskey, W., Stronge, J. H., Ward, T. J., Tucker, P. D., Howard, B., Lewis, K., & Hindman, J. L. (2006). *A comparison of National Board certified teachers and non-National Board certified teachers: Is there a difference in teacher effectiveness and student achievement?* Arlington, VA: National Board for Professional Teaching Standards.

McNeil, N. M. (2007). U-shaped development in math: 7-year-olds outperform 9-year-olds on equivalence problems. *Developmental Psychology, 43*(3), 687–695.

Medley, D. M., & Coker, H. (1987). The accuracy of principals' judgments of teacher performance. *Journal of Educational Research, 80*(4), 242–247.

Merton, R. K. (1948). The self-fulfilling prophecy. *Antioch Review, 8*, 193–210.

Merton, R. K (1968). *Social theory and social structure.* New York: Free Press.

Messick, S. (1989). Validity. In R. L. Linn (Ed.), *Educational measurement* (3rd ed., pp. 13–103). New York: American Council on Education and Macmillan.

Milanowski, A. (2004). The relationship between teacher performance evaluation scores and student achievement: Evidence from Cincinnati. *Peabody Journal of Education, 79*(4), 33–53.

Miller. G. A. (1956). The magical number seven plus or minus two: Some limits on our capacity for processing information. *Psychological Review, 63*(2), 81–97.

Monk, D. H. (1994). Subject area preparation of secondary mathematics and science teachers and student achievement. *Economics of Education Review, 13*(2), 125–145.

Muijs, D., Campbell, J., Kyriakides, L., & Robinson, W. (2005). Making the case for differentiated teacher effectiveness: An overview of research in four key areas. *School Effectiveness and School Improvement, 16*(1), 51–70.

Murnane, R.. (1975). *The impact of school resources on the learning of inner city children.* Cambridge, MA: Ballinger.

Murnane, R. J., & Cohen, D. K. (1986). Merit pay and the evaluation problem: Why most merit pay plans fail and a few survive. *Harvard Educational Review, 56*(1), 1–17.

Murnane, R. J., & Phillips, B. R. (1981a). Learning by doing, vintage, and selection: Three pieces of the puzzle relating teaching experience and teaching performance. *Economics of Education Review, 1*(4), 453–465.

Murnane, R. J., & Phillips, B. R. (1981b). What do effective teachers of inner-city children have in common? *Social Science Research, 10*(1), 83–100.

Murnane, R. J., Singer, J. D., Willett, J. B., Kemple, J. J., & Olsen, R. J. (1991). *Who will teach? Policies that matter.* Cambridge, MA: Harvard University Press.

Murray, H. G. (1983). Low inference classroom teaching behavior and student ratings of college teaching effectiveness. *Journal of Educational Psychology, 75*(1), 138–149.

Nakao, K. and Treas, J. (1990). *Computing 1989 occupational prestige scores.* General Social Survey Methodological Reports, #70. Chicago, IL: NORC.

National Commission on Excellence in Education. (1983). *A nation at risk: The imperative for educational reform.* Washington, DC: Author.

National Commission on Teaching and America's Future. (1996). *What matters most: Teaching for America's future.* New York: Author.

National Council of Teachers of Mathematics. (1989). *Curriculum and evaluation standards for school mathematics.* Reston, VA: Author.

National Council of Teachers of Mathematics. (1991). *Professional standards for school mathematics.* Reston, VA: Author.

National Council of Teachers of Mathematics. (2000). *Principles and standards for school mathematics.* Reston, VA: Author.

National Education Association. (2003). *Status of the American public school teacher 2000–2001.* Washington, DC: Author.

National Institute of Child Health and Human Development, Early Child Care Research Network (NICHD ECCRN). (2002). The relation of first grade classroom environment to structural classroom features, teacher, and student behaviors. *Elementary School Journal, 102*(5), 367–387.

National Research Council. (1996). *National science education standards.* Washington, DC: National Academy Press. Retrieved June 1, 2010, from http://www.nap.edu/openbook.php?record_id=4962

Neisser, U. (1963). The multiplicity of thought. *British Journal of Psychology, 54*(1), 1–14.

The New Teacher Project. (2007, July). *Teacher hiring, transfer and assignment in Chicago Public Schools.* New York: Author. Retrieved April 29, 2010, from http://www.tntp.org/files/TNTPAnalysis-Chicago.pdf

Newmann, F. M., and Associates. (1996). *Authentic achievement: Restructuring school for intellectual quality.* San Francisco: Jossey-Bass.

Newmann, F. M., Marks, H. M., & Gamoran, A. (1996). Authentic pedagogy and student performance. *American Journal of Education, 104*(4), 280–312.

Newton, X., Darling-Hammond, L., Haertel, E., & Thomas, E. (2010). Value-added modeling of teacher effectiveness; An exploration of stability across models and contexts. *Educational Policy Analysis Archives, 18* (23). Retrieved October 2, 2010, from http://epaa.asu.edu/ojs/article/view/810.

Nixon, L. A., & Robinson, M. D. (1999). The educational attainment of young women: Role model effects of female high school faculty. *Demography, 36*(2), 185–194.

Noell, G. H., & Burns, J. L. (2006). Value-added assessment of teacher preparation: An illustration of emerging technology. *Journal of Teacher Education, 57*(1), 37–50.

Nye, B., Konstantopoulos, S., & Hedges, L. V. (2004). How large are teacher effects? *Educational Evaluation and Policy Analysis, 26*(3), 237–257.

Pakarinen, E., Lerkkanen, M-K., Poikkeus, A-M., Kiuru, N., Siekkinen, M., Rasku-Puttonen, H., et al. (2010). A validation of the classroom assessment scoring system in Finnish kindergartens. *Early Education and Development, 21*(1), 95–124.

Pecheone, R. L., & Wei, R. C. (2009). *Review of "The widget effect: Our national failure to acknowledge and act on teacher differences."* Boulder and Tempe: Education and the Public Interest Center & Education Policy Research Unit. Retrieved 8/9/2010, from http://epicpolicy.org/thinktank/review-Widget-Effect

Piaget, J. (1926). *The language and thought of the child*. London: Routledge & Kegan Paul.

Pianta, R. C., La Paro, K., & Hamre, B. K. (2008). *Classroom Assessment Scoring System (CLASS)*. Baltimore: Paul H. Brookes.

Pianta, R. C., La Paro, K. M., Payne, C., Cox, M. J., & Bradley, R. (2002). The relation of kindergarten classroom environment to teacher, family, and school characteristics and child outcomes. *The Elementary School Journal, 102*(3), 225–238.

Podgursky, M. (2003). Fringe benefits. *Education Next, 3*(3), 71-76. Retrieved January 14, 2011, from http://educationnext.org/files/ednext20033_71.pdf.

Raudenbush, S. W. (1984). Magnitude of teacher expectancy effects on pupil IQ as a function of the credibility of expectancy inductions: A synthesis of findings from 18 experiments. *Journal of Educational Psychology, 76*(1), 85–97.

Raudenbush, S. W. (1994). Random effects models. In H. Cooper & L. V. Hedges (Eds.), *Handbook of research synthesis* (pp. 301–321). New York: Sage.

Ray, A., McCormack, T., & Evans, H. (2009). Value added in English schools. *Education Finance and Policy, 4*(4), 415–438.

Raymond, M. E., Fletcher, S. H., & Luque, J. A. (2001). *Teach for America: An evaluation of teacher differences and student outcomes in Houston, Texas*. Stanford University: Center for Research on Education Outcomes.

Rice, J. K. (2003). *Teacher quality: Understanding the effectiveness of teacher attributes*. Washington, DC: Economic Policy Institute.

Rice, J. K. (2009). Investing in human capital through teacher professional development. In D. Goldhaber & J. Hannaway (Eds.), *Creating a new teaching profession* (pp. 227–247). Washington, DC: The Urban Institute Press.

Rimm-Kaufman, S. E., La Paro, K. M., Downer, J. T., & Pianta, R. C. (2005). The contribution of classroom setting and quality of instruction to children's behavior in kindergarten classrooms. *The Elementary School Journal, 105*(4), 377–394.

Rist, R. (1970). Student social class and teacher expectations: The self-fulfilling prophecy in ghetto education. *Harvard Educational Review, 40*(3), 411–451.

Rivkin, S. G. (2009). The estimation of teacher value added as a determinant of performance pay.

In D. Goldhaber & J. Hannaway (Eds.), *Creating a new teaching profession* (pp. 181–193). Washington, DC: The Urban Institute Press.

Rivkin, S. G., Hanushek, E. A., & Kain, J. F. (2005). Teachers, schools, and academic achievement. *Econometrica, 73*(2), 417–458.

Rockoff, J. (2004). The impact of individual teachers on student achievement: Evidence from panel data. *American Economic Review, 94*(2), 247–252.

Rogers, C. R. (1969). *Freedom to learn.* Columbus, OH: Merrill.

Rosch, E. (1973). On the internal structure of perceptual and semantic categories. In T. E. Moore (Ed.), *Cognitive development and the acquisition of language* (pp. 112–144). New York: Academic Press.

Rosch, E. (1978). Principles of categorization. In E. Rosch & B. Lloyd (Eds.), *Cognition and categorization* (pp. 189–206). Hillsdale, NJ: Erlbaum.

Rosenholtz, S. J. (1989). *Teachers' workplace: The social organization of schools.* New York: Longman.

Rosenthal, R., & Jacobson, L. (1968a). *Pygmalion in the classroom: Teacher expectation and pupils' intellectual development.* New York: Holt, Rinehart and Winston.

Rosenthal, R., & Jacobson, L. (1968b). Pygmalion in the classroom. *The Urban Review, 3*(1), 16-20.

Ross, L., Lepper, M. R., & Hubbard, M. (1975). Perseverance in self-perception and social perception: biased attributional processes in the debriefing paradigm. *Journal of Personality and Social Psychology, 32*(5), 880–802.

Rotter, J. (1990). Internal versus external control of reinforcement: A case history of a variable. *American Psychologist, 45*(4), 489–493.

Rowan, B., Camburn, E., & Correnti, R. (2004). Using teacher logs to measure the enacted curriculum in large-scale surveys: Insights from the Study of Instructional Improvement. *Elementary School Journal, 105*(1) 75–102.

Rowan, B., Chiang, F.-S., & Miller, R. J. (1997). Using research on employees' performance to study the effects of teachers on students' achievement. *Sociology of Education, 70*(4), 256–284.

Rowan, B., & Correnti, R. (2009). Studying reading instruction with teacher logs: Lessons from the study of instructional improvement. *Educational Researcher, 38*(2), 120–131.

Rowan, B., Correnti, R., & Miller, R. J. (2002). What large-scale, survey research tells us about teacher effects on student achievement: Insights from the Prospects Study of elementary schools. *Teachers College Record, 104*(8), 1525–1567.

Rowan, B., Correnti, R., Miller, R., & Camburn, E. (2009). School improvement by design: Lessons from a study of comprehensive school reform programs. In G. Sykes, B. L. Schneider, and D. N. Plank (Eds.), *Handbook of education policy research.* Washington, DC: American Educational Research Association/Routledge.

Rowan, B., & Miller, R. J. (2007). Organizational strategies for promoting instructional change: Implementation dynamics in schools working with comprehensive school reform providers. *American Educational Research Journal, 44*(2), 252–297.

Rushton, S., Morgan, J., & Richard, M. (2007). Teacher's Myers-Briggs personality profiles: Identifying effective teacher personality traits. *Teaching and Teacher Education, 23*(4), 432–441.

Sanders, W. L. (2000). Value-added assessment from student achievement data: Opportunities and hurdles. *Journal of Personnel Evaluation in Education 14*(4), 329–339.

Sanders, W. L., Ashton, J. J., and Wright, S. P. (2005). *Comparison of the effects of NBPTS certified teachers with other teachers on the rate of student academic progress.* Arlington, VA: National Board for Professional Teaching Standards.

Sanders, W. L., & Horn, S. P. (1995). The Tennessee Value-Added Assessment System (TVAAS): Mixed model methodology in educational assessment. In A. J. Shrinkfield & D. Stufflebeam (Eds.), *Teacher evaluation: Guide to effective practice* (pp. 337–350). Boston: Kluwer.

Sanders, W. L., & Horn, S. P. (1998). Research findings from the Tennessee value-added assessment system (TVAAS) database: Implications for educational evaluation and research. *Journal of Personnel Evaluation in Education, 12* (3), 247–256.

Sanders, W. L, & Rivers, J. C. (1996). *Cumulative and residual effects of teachers on future student academic achievement.* Knoxville: University of Tennessee Value-Added Assessment Center. Retrieved 10/21/2009 from http://www.cgp.upenn.edu/pdf/Sanders_Rivers-TVASS_teacher %20effects.pdf

Schacter, J., & Thum, Y. M. (2004). Paying for high- and low-quality teaching. *Economics of Education Review, 23*(4): 411–430.

Scheerens, J. (1992) *Effective schooling: research, theory and practice.* London: Cassell.

Schoenfeld, A. H. (2004). The math wars. *Educational Policy, 18*(1), 253–286.

Schwerdt, G., & Wuppermann, A. C. (2009). *Is traditional teaching really all that bad? A within-student between-subject approach.* CESifo Working Paper No. 2634. Munich: CESifo. Retrieved August 10, 2010, from http://www.ifo-geschaeftsklima.info/pls/guestci/download/CESifo%20Working%20Papers%202009/CESifo%20Working%20Papers%20April%202009/cesifo1_wp2634.pdf

Shulman, L. S. (1986). Those who understand: Knowledge growth in teaching. *Educational Researcher, 15*(2), 4–14.

Silver, E. A., Mesa, V. M., Morris, K. A., Star, J. R., & Benken, B. M. (2009). An analysis of lessons submitted by teachers seeking NBPTS certification. *American Educational Research Journal, 46*(2), 501–531.

Simons, D. J., & Chabris, C. F. (1999) Gorillas in our midst: sustained inattentional blindness for dynamic events. *Perception 28*(9), 1059–1074.

Sireci, S. G. (2007). On validity theory and test validation. *Educational Researcher, 36,* 477–481.

Skinner, E. A., & Belmont, M. J. (1993). *Journal of Educational Psychology, 85*(4), 571–581.

Sloman, S. A. (1996). The empirical case for two systems of reasoning. *Psychological Bulletin, 119*(1), 3–22.

Smith, A., Jussim, L., & Eccles, J. (1999). Do self-fulfilling prophecies accumulate, dissipate, or remain stable over time? *Journal of Personality and Social Psychology, 77*(3), 548–565.

Smith, T. W. (2007). *Job satisfaction in the United States.* NORC, University of Chicago. Retrieved 12/30/2009 from http://www.norc.org/NR/rdonlyres/2874B40B-7C50-4F67-A6B2-26-BD3B06EA04/0/JobSatisfactionintheUnitedStates.pdf

Snow, R. E. (1969). Unfinished Pygmalion. *Contemporary Psychology, 14*(4), 197–199.

Snow, R. E. (1995). Pygmalion and intelligence? *Current Directions in Psychological Science, 4*(6), 169–171.

Soar, R., & Soar, R. (1979). Emotional climate and management. In P. Peterson & H. Walberg (Eds.), *Research on teaching: Concepts, findings, and implications,* (pp. 97–119). Berkeley, CA: McCutchen.

Sparks, R., & Lipka, R. P. (1992). Characteristics of master teachers: Personality factors, self-concept, locus of control, and pupil ideology. *Journal of Personnel and Evaluation in Education, 5*(3), 303–311.

Spitz, H. H. (1999). Beleaguered Pygmalion: A history of the controversy over claims that teacher expectancy raises intelligence. *Intelligence, 27*(3), 199–234.

Stanovich, K. E., & West, R. F. (2000). Individual differences in reasoning: Implications for the rationality debate. *Behavioral and Brain Sciences, 23*(5), 645–665.

Stecher, B. M., Borko, H., Kuffner, K. L., Wood, A. C., Arnold, S. C., Gilbert, M. L., and Dorman E. H. (2005). *Using classroom artifacts to measure instructional practices in middle school mathematics: A two-state field test* (CSE Technical Report No. 662). Los Angeles: University of California, National Center for Research on Evaluation, Standards and Student Testing (CRESST).

Sternberg, R. J., & Horvath, J. A. (1995). A prototype view of expert teaching. *Educational Researcher, 24*(6), 9–17.

Strong, M. (2009). *Effective teacher induction and mentoring: Assessing the evidence.* New York: Teachers College Press.

Strong, M., Gargani, J., & Hacifazlioğlu, Ö. (2011). Do we know a successful teacher when we see one? Experiments in the identification of effective teachers. *Journal of Teacher Education, 64*(4), 1–16.

Summers, A., & Wolfe, B. (1977). Do schools make a difference? *American Economic Review, 67*(4), 639–652.

Tabachnick, B. R., & Zeichner, K. M. (1984). The impact of the student teaching experience on the development of teacher perspectives. *Journal of Teacher Education, 35*(6), 28–36.

Taylor, M. C. (1992). Expectancies and the perpetuation of racial inequality. In P. D. Blanck (Ed.), *Interpersonal expectancies* (pp. 88–124). New York: Cambridge University Press.

Temin, P. (2002). Teacher quality and the future of America. NBER Working Paper, 8898. Cambridge, MA.

Thomas, W. I., & Thomas, D. S. (1928). *The child in America: Behavior problems and programs.* New York: Knopf.

Tickle, L. (1999). Teacher self-appraisal and appraisal of self. In R. P. Lipka & T. M. Brinthaupt (Eds.), *The role of self in teacher development* (pp. 121–141). Albany, NY: State University of New York Press.

Treiman, D. (1977). *Occupational prestige in comparative perspective.* New York: Academic Press.

Tucker, P. D., Stronge, J. H., Gareis, C. R., & Beers, C. S. (2003). The efficiency of portfolios for teacher evaluation and professional development: Do they make a difference? *Educational Administration Quarterly, 39*(5), 572–602.

U.S. Department of Education. (1997). *Indicator 34: Starting salaries of college graduates, recent college graduates survey (1977–90) and 1993 Baccalaureate and Beyond longitudinal study, first follow-up.* Washington, DC: National Center for Education Statistics.

U.S. Department of Education. (1997). *America's Teachers: Profile of a Profession, 1993–94.* NCES 97-460. Washington, DC: National Center for Education Statistics.

U.S. Department of Education. (2002). *Meeting the highly qualified teachers challenge: The secretary's annual report on teacher quality.* Washington, DC: Government Printing Office.

Vygotsky, L. S. (1987). Thinking and speech. In R. W. Rieber & A. S. Carton (Eds.), *The collected works of L. S. Vygotsky.* Vol. 1: Problems of general psychology. New York: Plenum Press. (Originally published 1934)

Wachtel, H. K. (1998). Student evaluation of college teaching effectiveness: A brief review. *Assessment and Evaluation in Higher Education, 23*(2), 191–212.

Walker, R. J. (2008). Twelve characteristics of an effective teacher: A longitudinal, qualitative, quasi-research study of in-service and pre-service teachers' opinions. *Educational Horizons, 87*(1), 61–68.

Walls, R. T., Nardi, A. H., Von Minden, A. M., & Hoffinan, N. (2002). The characteristics of effective and ineffective teachers. *Teacher Education Quarterly 29(1),* 39–48.

Walsh, K. C. (2001). *Teacher certification reconsidered: Stumbling for quality.* Baltimore: The Abell Foundation. Retrieved October 10, 2009, from http://www.abell.org/pubsitems/ed_cert_1101.pdf

Walsh, K. (2002). Positive spin: The evidence for traditional teacher certification, reexamined. *Education Next, 2*(1), 79–84.

Walsh, K., & Jacobs, S. (2007). *Alternative certification isn't alternative.* Washington, DC: Thomas B. Fordham Institute.

Walsh, K., & Podgursky, M. (2001). Teacher certification reconsidered: Stumbling for quality. A rejoinder. Baltimore: The Abell Foundation. Retrieved March 18, 2010, from http://abell. org/pubsitems/ed_cert_rejoinder_1101.pdf

Wason, P. C. (1960). On the failure to eliminate hypotheses in a conceptual task. *Quarterly Journal of Experimental Psychology, 12,* 129–140.

Wayne, A., & Youngs, P. (2003). Teacher characteristics and student achievement gains: A review. *Review of Educational Research, 73*(1), 89–122.

Webster, W. J., & Mendro, R. L. (1995). Evaluation for improved school level decision-making and productivity. *Studies in Educational Evaluation, 21*(4), 361–399.

Weinstein, R. S., & McKown, C. (1998). Expectancy effects in "context": Listening to the voices of students and teachers. In J. Brophy (Ed.), *Advances in research on teaching* (Vol. 7, pp. 215–242). Greenwich, CT: JAI.

Weisberg, D., Sexton, S., Mulhern, J., & Keeling, D. (2009). *The widget effect: Our national failure to acknowledge and act on teacher differences.* Brooklyn, NY: The New Teacher Project. Retrieved August 23, 2010 from http://widgeteffect.org/

Wenglinsky, H. (2000). *How teaching matters: Bringing the classroom back into discussions of teacher quality.* Princton, NJ: ETS.

Wenglinsky, H. (2002). How schools matter: The link between teacher classroom practices and student academic performance. *Education Policy Analysis Archives, 10*(12). Retrieved February 19, 2010 from http://epaa.asu.edu/epaa/v10n12/

West, C., & Anderson, T. (1976). The question of preponderant causation in teacher expectancy research. *Review of Educational Research, 46*(4), 613–630.

Wilkerson, D. J., Manatt, R. P., Rogers, M. A., & Maughan, R. (2000). Validation of student, principal, and self-ratings in 360° feedback® for teacher evaluation. *Journal of Personnel Evaluation in Education, 14*,(2) 179–192.

Wilson, S. M., & Floden, R. E. (2003). *Creating effective teachers: Concise answers for hard questions (Addendum to the report, "Teacher preparation research: Current knowledge, gaps, and recommendations.").* Washington, DC: American Association of Colleges for Teacher Education. ERIC Document. Retrieved October 11, 2009, from http://eric.ed.gov/ERICDocs/data/ericdocs2sql/content_storage_01/0000019b/80/1b/0a/48.pdf

Wilson, S. M., Floden, R. E., & Ferrini-Mundy, J. (2001). *Teacher preparation research: Current knowledge, gaps, and recommendations.* Seattle, WA: Center for the Study of Teaching and Policy. Retrieved February 10, 2010, from http://depts.washington.edu/ctpmail/PDFs/TeacherPrep-WFFM-02-2001.pdf

Wineburg, S. S. (1987). The self-fulfillment of the self-fulfilling prophecy: A critical appraisal. *Educational Researcher 16*(1), 28–40.

Wise, A. (2005). Establishing teaching as a profession: The essential role of professional accreditation. *Journal of Teacher Education, 56*(4), 318–331.

Witcher, A. E., Onwuegbuzie, A. J., & Minor, L. C. (2001). Characteristics of effective teachers: Perceptions of preservice teachers. *Research in the Schools, 8*(2), 45–57.

Witty, P. (1947). An analysis of the personality traits of the effective teacher. *The Journal of Educational Research, 40*(9), 662–671.

Wright, S. P. (2008). *Estimating educational effects using analysis of covariance with measurement error.* Paper presented at CREATE's National Evaluation Institute October 9-11. Wilmington, NC. Retrieved September 25, 2010, from http://createconference.org/documents/archive/2008/2008wright.pdf

Wright, S. P., Horn, S. P., & Sanders, W. L. (1997). Teacher and classroom context effects on student achievement: Implications for teacher evaluation. *Journal of Personnel Evaluation in Education, 1*(1), 57–67.

Index

Note: Page numbers followed by an "f" or "t" indicate figures or tables, respectively; the letter "n" indicates a note number.

Aaronson, D., 8n29, 23n24, 47n151
Abell Foundation, 33n73
Academic preparation, of teachers, 22–27
Accountability, teacher effectiveness and, 105
Achievement gap, Black-White, 36
AFQT (Armed Forces Qualifying Test), 2n13
Alexander, E. R., 69n36
All Things Considered (radio show), excerpt
    from, 85–87
Allinder, R. M., 37n100
Alonzo, A. C., 75n54–55
Alternatively certified (AC) programs, 27
Ambady, N., 90n16–17, 91n18
American Association for the Advancement
    of Science (AAAS), 16, 109n18
American Federation of Teachers (AFT),
    3, 52n3
America's Teacher Corps, 10
Amrein-Beardsley, A., 80n75
Anderson, T., 38n107, 38n111
Andrew, M. D., 39n118, 40n121
Anthony, E., 20n11, 64n31
Armed Forces Qualifying Test (AFQT), 2n13
Armor, D., 37n96
Arnold, S. C., 75n54

Artifacts, of teaching, 73–75
Aschbacher, P., 74n50
Ashton, J. J., 22n15
Ashton, P., 37n97
Aslam, M., 45n145
Attitude, as teacher attribute, 13–15, 36–38
Attributes. *See* Teacher attributes
Audit system, 43, 114n133
Authentic pedagogy, 74

Bacolod, M. P., 1–2n10, 2n11
Baker, E. L., 79n70, 82n89
Ball, D., 29n51, 62
Ballou, D., 10n40, 73n48, 80n72, 80n74
Bandura, A., 37n94
Barbarin, O. A., 58n20
Barnes, C. A., 76n58, 77n61
Barnes, D., 75n54
Baron, R., 36n86
Barron's College Admissions Selector, 23
Barron's Educational Series, 3n17
Barrow, L., 8n29, 23n25, 47n151
Barton, P. E., 79n70, 82n89
Beard, R., 44n141
Bee, M., 3n18

Beers, C. S., 73n49

Beginning Educator Support and Training (BEST) Program, 72

Behavior management, as CLASS dimension, 58, 59t

Belief perseverance, 89

Beliefs, as teacher attribute, 36–38

Belmont, M. J., 17n25

Benjamin, D. J., 91n19

Benken, B. M., 74n52–53

Berliner, D., 13n2, 25n35–36

Berman, P., 37n96

Bernieri, F. J., 90n17

Berry, B., 34n76

BEST (Beginning Educator Support and Training) Program, 72

Betts, J., 81n80

Betts, J. R., 19n5, 23n27, 29n53

Bias
  cognitive operations and, 88–90
  confirmation, 88
  hindsight, 89
  perceptual, 36

Black-White achievement gap, 36

Blanton, L., 13n3

Blau, P., 4n23

Blindness, inattentional, 88

Blume, R. A., 14n12

Blunk, M. L., 62n26, 62n28

Bommer, W. H., 69n35

Borko, H., 75n54, 75n55

Borman, G., 41n125

Boston, M., 42n130

Boyd, D., 26n39, 60n24, 62n25

Bradley, R., 58n17

Brandt, C., 69n32, 69n34

Braun, C., 38n107

Braun, H., 79n70–71

Brewer, D., 8n29, 9n32–33, 19n3, 23n23, 23n26, 34n76, 36n87, 39n119, 40n120

British Education Reform Act (1988), 1n9, 107n9

Brophy, J., 38n107, 53n5

Brown, J., 28n46

Brown, N., 14n9

Brown-Sims, M., 69n32, 69n34

Bryant, D., 58n20, 59n21, 60n22

Buckeye Institute, 31n66

Burchinal, M., 59n21, 60n22

Burns, J. L., 47n154

Burstein, L., 76n57

California Department of Education, 43n135

California Learning Assessment System (CLAS), 29, 43

Camburn, E., 76n58, 77n60–61

Campbell, E. Q., 9n31, 39n115

Campbell, R. J., 17n28, 17n30, 82n86

Canada, G., 105

Carlgren, I., 17n29

Carnegie Task Force on Teaching, 53, 53n7

Carr, M., 23n28–29, 31n68

Cavalluzzo, L. C., 20n7, 31n63

Center for the Advanced Study of Teaching and Learning (CASTL), 97

Center to Support Excellence in Teaching, 60n23

Certification
  programs for, 29
  qualifications and, 22–32
  student achievement and, 19–22
  teacher effectiveness and, 32–35

Chabris, C. F., 88n5

Chaiken, S., 89n11

Chait, R., 12n1

Channel capacity, 88

Charalambous, C. Y., 62n26, 62n28

Chiang, F.-S., 29n52

Christensen-Szalanski, J. J., 89n9

Chudowsky, N., 79nn70–71

Clare, L., 74n50

CLAS (California Learning Assessment System), 29

CLASS (Classroom Assessment Scoring System), 58–60, 61, 85, 97–98, 102
dimensions of, 58, 59t

Classroom observation, 41–43, 53–55, 83. *See also* CLASS (Classroom Assessment Scoring System)
cautions when undertaking, 89
cognitive operations influencing, 88–90
Danielson's protocol for. *See* Framework for Teaching (observation protocol)
Protocol for Language Arts Teaching Observation, 60–62
scoring system for. *See* CLASS (Classroom Assessment Scoring System)

Classroom Observation System for First Graders (COS-1), 58

Classroom organization, in CLASS, 58, 59t

Clements, S. K., 30n58, 43n134

Clewell, B. C., 35n79

Clifford, R., 59n21

Climate of classroom, as CLASS dimension, 58, 59t

Clotfelter, C., 21n12, 23n21, 23n28, 28n48

Cobb, C. D., 39n118, 40n121

Coble, C. R., 20n6

Cognitive operations, 88–89
System 1 vs. System 2, 89–90

Cognitive operations, observations influenced by, 88–90

Cohen, D. K., 10n41, 29n56, 43n137, 52n4, 53n6, 62n25

Cohen, J., 60n24

Cohort-to-cohort change models, value-added modeling vs., 79

Coker, H., 70n40

Coleman, J. S., 9n31, 39n115

Combs, A. W., 14n12

Concept development, 58, 59t

Confirmation bias, 88

Conry-Oseguera, P., 37n96

Consortium for Policy Research in Education (CPRE), 41, 76

Constantine, J., 27n41

Contextual value-added (CVA) models, 80

Cooney, S., 45n146

Cooper, H., 36n86, 38n107

Corcoran, S. P., 1n5, 1n8, 27n42, 27n43

Correa, V., 13n3

Correnti, R., 31n62, 76n58, 77n59, 77n62–63

COS-1 (Classroom Observation System for First Graders), 58

Counts, G. S., 4n24

Cox, M., 37n96, 58n17

Cronbach, L. J., 54n9

Cunningham, M., 4n26, 6n27

Danielson, C., 41n123, 54. *See also* Framework for Teaching (observation protocol)

Darling-Hammond, L., 10n39, 18n1, 20n8, 25n33–34, 33n75, 34n76–77, 39n117, 79n70, 81n79, 82n89

Davis, D. D., 89n8

Decker, P. T., 10n38, 24n32

Dee, T. S., 35nn80–82, 82n85

Deke, J., 27n41

Deliberate thought process, 89

Dillon, S., 82n91

Doda, N., 37n96

Dolton, P., 3n18

Dorman, E. H., 75n54

Downer, J. T., 58n20, 60n22

Downey, C. J., 69n33, 91n20

Dublin, T., 1n1

Duncan, A., 50

Duncan, O. D., 4n23

Dusek, J., 38n107

Early, D., 59n21

Early Child Care Research Network, 58n18

Eccles, J., 38n111–12

Education Finance and Policy, 79n70

Educational Researcher, 39

Effectiveness. *See* Teacher effectiveness

Ehrenberg, R., 23n23, 36n87, 39n119, 40n120

Eide, E., 9n32

Elashoff, J. D., 38n107

Emotional support, in CLASS, 58, 59t

English, F. W., 69n33, 91n20

English Language Arts (ELA), 60–61

English Language Learner (ELL), 61–62

Epstein, S., 89n11

Equality of Educational Opportunity
    (Coleman), 8

Etzioni, A., 9n36

Evaluation. *See individually named*
    measurement instruments; Teacher
    evaluation

Evans, H., 80n76

Evans, W. N., 1n5, 1n8

Everton, T., 4n26, 6n27

Evidence
    scientific, 39
    of teacher effectiveness, implications
        from, 104–5
    of teacher qualifications, 48–50, 83–84

Experiments, in teacher rating
    implications from, 102–3
    methodologies and findings, 90–102
    rationale for, 90–91

Explicit Strategy Instruction, 61

Falch, J., 49n157

Ferguson, R. F., 28n46, 36n85, 39n116

Fernstermacher, G. D., 17n22–23, 24n30

Ferrini-Mundy, J., 19n2

Fetler, M., 17n26

Finn, J., 38n107

Fischhoff, B., 89n9

Floden, R. E., 19n2

Florida League of Teachers, 37

Follman, J., 78n67

Ford Foundation, 29

Framework for Teaching (observation
    protocol), 41, 54–55
    evaluation systems based on, 56t–57t
    student achievement and, 55
    teaching domains in, 54

Frase, L. E., 69n33, 91n20

Frederick, S., 89n11, 90n13–14

Frome, P., 45n146

Gallagher, H. A., 31n67, 42n128

Gamoran, A., 74n51

Gareis, C. R., 73n49

Gargani, J., 87n1

Gatlin, S. J., 20n8, 34n77

Gender, as teacher attribute, 36, 82

General Social Survey (GSS), 4

Getzels, J. W., 36n90

Giampietro, P. J., 39n118, 40n121

Gilbert, M. L., 75n54

Glazerman, S., 10n38, 10n42, 24n32

Goddard, R. D., 37n95, 37n99

Goe, L., 18n1

Goldhaber, D., 8n29, 9n32–33, 10n41–42,
    19n3, 20n11, 23n26, 34n76, 36n87,
    46n149, 64n31, 81nn83–84

Good, T., 38n107, 53n5

Goodson, I., 9n34

Graham, P. A., 35n79

Gray, H. M., 90n16

Grider, M., 27n41

Grossman, P., 26n39, 60n24, 62n25

Growth models, value-added modeling vs.,
    79

GSS (General Social Survey), 4

Guitton, G., 76n57

Hacifazlioğlu, Ö., 87n1
Haertel, E., 79n70, 81n79, 82n89
Hallgren, K., 27n41
Hamilton, L., 80n75, 81n80
Hammerness, K., 60n24, 62n25
Hamre, B. K., 58n16, 58n19, 97nn25–26
Han, B., 81nn81–82, 94n23
Han, S. W., 77n60
Hansen, A., 4n26, 6n27
Hansen, M., 46n146, 81nn83–84
Hanushek, E. A., 3n18, 8nn29–30, 8n30,
        23n29, 28n45, 28n47, 30n59, 31n65,
        32nn69–70, 35n83, 47n152
Harber, K. D., 38n105, 38n113
Harbison, R. W., 30n59
Hardman, M., 13n3
Hargreaves, A., 9n34, 10n37
Hargreaves, L., 4n26, 6n27
Harlem Children's Zone (HCZ), 105
Harris, D. N., 22n16, 23n28–29, 28n49,
        29n54, 70n39, 70n43, 71n44, 81n78
Hastie, R., 89n9
Hawk, P., 20n6
Hawkins, S. A., 89n9
Heck, R. H., 45n147
Hedges, L. V., 8n29, 47n155
Heilig, J. V., 20n8, 34n77
Heneman, H. G., 41n124, 55n14
Heneman, R. L., 69n35
Hess, J., 69n32, 69n34
High School and Beyond (longitudinal study
        dataset), 23, 110n22
Hill, H. C., 28, 29, 29n51, 29n56,
        43n137, 62n26
Hindman, J. L., 21n13, 22n14, 37n98
Hindsight bias, 89
Hobson, C. J., 9n31, 39n115
Hodge, R. W., 4n23
Hofer, M. A., 38n106
Hoffman, N., 14n7

Holtzapple, E., 42n127
Holtzman, D. J., 20n8, 34n77
Hopper, B., 4n26, 6n27
Horn, S. P., 78n68, 80n73, 91n21
Horvath, J. A., 15n15, 15n17
Howard, B., 21n13, 22n14, 37n98
Howes, C., 59n21, 60n22
Hoy, A. W., 37n95, 37n99
Hoy, W. K., 37n95, 37n99
Hoyle, E., 9n35
Hubbard, M., 89n7
Hyland, T., 14n10

Illinois Goals Assessment Program, 74
Inattentional blindness, 88
Ingersoll, R. M., 1n4, 3n16
Instructional learning formats, as CLASS
        dimension, 58, 59t
Instructional Quality Assessment (IQA), 42
Instructional support, in CLASS, 58, 59t
Interstate New Teacher Assessment and
        Support Consortium (INTASC), 9, 54
Intuitive thought process, 89
Iowa Tests of Basic Skills, 74
IQ Tests, 38

Jackson, P. W., 36n90
Jacob, B. A., 69n37, 70nn41–42
Jacobs, S., 26n40
Jacobson, L., 36n84, 37n101
James, W., 89n10
Jennings, J. L., 27n42, 27n43
Jepsen, C., 19n4
Job satisfaction, 6–7, 7t, 8t
Johnson, J. L., 69n35
Johnson-Laird, P. N., 89n10
Jones, E. E., 38n106
Jones, R., 75n56
Junker, B., 42n130
Jussim, L., 38n105, 38n111, 38n113

Kahneman, D., 89n11, 90n13, 90n15
Kain, J. F., 8n29, 23n29, 35n83, 47n152
Kane, M., 54n9
Kane, T. J., 8n29, 20n9, 25n37, 26n38, 55n15
Kannapel, P. J., 30n58, 43n134
Kapitula, L. R., 62n29
Keeling, D., 82n87
Kemple, J. J., 1n6, 2n14
Kimball, S. M., 41n125–26, 55n14
King, N., 37n96
Kingdon, G., 45n145
Kiuru, N., 60n22
Koedel, C., 81n80
Koenig, J., 79nn70–71
Konold, T., 60n22
Konstantopoulos, S., 8n29, 47n155
Koretz, D. M., 80n75
Korthagen, F. A. J., 15n14
Kottemann, J. E., 89n8
Kuffner, K. L., 75n54
Kuhel, K., 13n3
Kunda, Z., 88n4
Kupermintz, H., 80n75
Kyriakides, L., 17n30, 82n86

La Paro, K., 58nn16–17, 60n22, 97nn25–26
LA Times. See Los Angeles Times
Laczko-Kerr, I., 25n3, 25n36
Ladd, H., 21n12, 23n21, 23n28, 28n48,
    79n70, 82n89
Lakdawalla, D., 3n19–20
Language modeling, as CLASS dimension,
    58, 59t
Lankford, H., 26n39
Lasater, B., 45n146
Lasley, T. J., 14n7
Le, V-N., 81n80
Learning Mathematics for Teaching, 62n27
Lefgren, L., 69n37, 70nn41–42
Lepper, M. R., 89n7

Lerkkanen, M-K., 60n22
Lewis, J. M., 62n26, 62n28
Lewis, K., 21n13, 22n14, 37n98
Linn, R. L., 79n70, 82n89
Lipka, R. P., 13n5
Literacy hour program, 44, 115n140
LoCasale-Crouch, J., 60n22
Lockwood, J. R., 80n75, 81nn79–82, 94n23
Loeb, S., 10n42, 26n39, 60n24, 62n25
Lohse, G. L., 89n8
Los Angeles Times, ix, 49, 78–79, 79n69,
    82, 86, 87, 91
Louis, T. A., 80n75

Machin, S., 44n139, 44n140
Mack, A., 88n5
Mackenzie, S. B., 69n35
Madon, S. J., 38n112
Manatt, R. P., 71n45
Manski, C. F., 1n7
Marcoulides, G. A., 45n147
Marks, H. M., 74n51
Martinez, F., 75n54
Martinez, J. F., 81n80
Mashburn, A. J., 58n20
Maslow, A. H., 14n11
Mathematical knowledge for teaching
    (MKT), 62
Mathematical Policy Associates, 10n38,
    108n38
Mathematical Policy Research (MPR), 26–27
Mathematical Quality of Instruction
    (MQI), 62–64
    elements of, 63t
    sections of, 62
Mathers, C., 69n32, 69n34
Matsumura, L. C., 42n130
Maughan, R., 71n45
Mayer, D. P., 10n38, 24n32, 77n64
McCaffrey, D., 80n75, 81nn79–82, 94n23

McClam, S., 75nn54–55
McColskey, W., 21n13, 22n14, 37n98
McCormack, T., 80n76
McDonnell, J., 13n3
McDonnell, L., 37n96, 76n57
McIntyre, D., 4n26, 6n27
McKown, C., 38n106
McLaughlin, M. W., 37n96
McNally, S., 44nn139–40
McNeil, N. M., 50n158
McPartland, J., 9n31, 39n115
Measurement instruments. *See individually
    named measurement instruments*
Measures of Effective Teaching (MET),
    54n13, 60, 62, 78
Medley, D. M., 70n40
Mendro, R. L., 17n27
Merrill, L., 1n4, 3n16
Merton, R. K., 38n108
Mesa, V. M., 74n52–53
Messick, S., 54n9
MET (Measures of Effective Teaching),
    54n13, 60, 62, 78
Mihaly, K., 81n79
Milanowski, A., 41n124, 42n129, 55n14
Milanowski, A. T., 41n126
Miller, G. A., 88n6
Miller, R., 29n52, 31n62, 76n58
Minor, L. C., 14n7
Mirocha, J., 76n57
Models/Modeling
    contextual value-added models, 80
    language, as CLASS dimension, 58, 59t
    passive vs. active roles, 35
    value-added. *See* Value-added modeling
        (VAM)
Moncure, S., 75nn54–55
Monk, D. H., 22n17, 29n55
Mood, A. M., 9n31, 39n115
Morehead, P., 14n9

Morgan, J., 37n92
Morris, K. A., 74nn52–53
Motivated reasoning, 88
MQI. *See* Mathematical Quality of
    Instruction (MQI)
Muijs, R. D., 17n30, 82n86
Mulhern, J., 82n87
Murnane, R., 69n38
Murnane, R. J., 1n6, 2n14, 10n41, 28n44,
    30n60
Murray, H. G., 13n5
Myers-Briggs Type Indicator, 36–37n91

Nakao, K., 4n25
Nardi, A. H., 14n7
National Assessment of Educational Progress
    (NAEP), 13n2, 22, 29, 44n138
National Board Certification, 20, 21, 22, 34,
    110n10
National Board for Professional Teaching
    Standards (NBPTS), 9, 20, 21, 52n2, 53,
    72n47, 74, 110n10
National Bureau of Economic Research, 19
National Center for Alternative Certification
    (NCAC), 24n31
National Center for Education Statistics
    (NCES), 1n3
National Center for Research on Evaluation,
    Standards and Student Testing
    (CRESST), 74
National Commission on Excellence in
    Education, 53n7
National Commission on Teaching and
    America's Future (NCTAF), 33n71–72
National Comprehensive Center for Teacher
    Quality, 54n10
National Council for Accreditation of Teacher
    Education (NCATE), 9, 52n1
National Council of Teacher Quality
    (NCTQ), 33, 112n74

National Council of Teachers of Mathematics
  (NCTM), 9, 16nn18–20, 109n18
  content standards, 43, 44n143, 77n65,
    114n136
National Education Association, 1n2, 11n43
National Educational Longitudinal Study of
  1988 (NELS:88), 23, 36, 110n25
National Institute of Child Health and
  Human Development (NICHD),
  58, 58n18
National Literacy Project, 44
National Longitudinal Surveys (NLS), 36n88
  of young men (NLS-YM), 2n12
  of young women (NLS-YW), 2n12
  of youth-79 (NLS-Y79), 2n12
National Opinion Research Center
  (NORC), 4
National Research Council (NRC), 16,
  44n144, 109n18
National Science Foundation (NSF), 16, 76
Neisser, U., 89n10
NELS:88 (National Educational Longitudinal
  Study of 1988), 23, 36, 110n25
New Teacher Project, 71n46
New York City Teaching Fellows (NYCTF),
  24, 25, 26, 33
Newman, A. J., 14n12
Newmann, F. M., 74n51
Newmann and Associates, 74n51
Newton, X., 79n70, 81n79
Nixon, L. A., 36n89
NLS. See National Longitudinal Surveys
  (NLS)
No Child Left Behind (NCLB), 12, 13,
  35, 108n1
Noell, G. H., 47n154
Nye, B., 8n29, 47n155

Obama, B., ix, 11
O'Brien, D. M., 23n29, 35n83

Observation. See Classroom observation;
  Framework for Teaching (observation
  protocol)
Occupation rankings
  prestige, 4–5, 5t, 6t
  satisfaction, 6–7, 7t, 8t
Odden, A., 41n124, 55n14
Oliva, M., 69n32, 69n34
Olsen, R. J., 1n6, 2n14
Onwuegbuzie, A. J., 14n7
Organization, classroom, in CLASS, 58, 59t
Ormseth, T., 76n57

Paige, R., 39
Pakarinen E., 60n22
Papanastasiou, C., 45n147
Parent education level, 50
Pascal, A, 37n96
Pauly, E., 37n96
Payne, C., 58n17
Pecheone, R. L., 82n88
Pedagogical content knowledge, 111n50
Pedagogical practice studies, 40–41
  classroom observation, 41–43
  student surveys, 45
  teacher surveys, 43–45
Pedagogy, authentic, 74
Perceptual bias, 36
Perceptual phenomena, teacher observation
  instruments and, 89
Perda, D., 1n9
Performance pay, 105
Performance ratings, 70, 71
Performance rubrics, for quality teaching
  measures, 64, 65t–68t
Personality, as teacher attribute, 13–15, 36–38
Peterson, M., 42n130
Phelps, G. C., 62n26, 62n28
Phillips, B. R., 28n44
Piaget, J., 89n10

Pianta, R. C., 58nn16–17, 58n19, 59n21, 60n22, 97nn25–26

PLATO (Protocol for Language Arts Teaching Observation), 60–62

Player, D., 27n41

Podgursky, M., 3n22, 10n40, 32n69, 33n75

Podsakoff, P. M., 69n35

Poikkeus, A-M., 60n22

Portfolios, 72–73

Poston, W. K., Jr., 69n33, 91n20

Poverty status, 50

Praxis III, 54n11, 117n11

Preparation program, 24–27

Prestige rankings, of different occupations, 4–5, 5t, 6t

Productivity, as CLASS dimension, 58, 59t

Professional development
    funding for, 105
    level of, 29–30

Professionalism/Professionalization, 9

Prospects National Longitudinal Study, 31n61

Protocol for Language Arts Teaching Observation (PLATO), 60–62

Pygmalion in the Classroom (Rosenthal & Jacobson), 37–38

Qualifications. *See* Teacher qualifications

Quality
    of feedback, as CLASS dimension, 58, 59t
    of teaching. *See* Teacher quality

Race, as teacher attribute, 35–36, 82

"Race to the Top" (slogan), 11

Racial stereotyping, 36

RAND Corporation, 49, 76, 79

Rapid Assessment of Teacher Effectiveness (RATE), 98–102, 103

Rasku-Puttonen, H., 60n22

RATE (Rapid Assessment of Teacher Effectiveness), 98–102

Rating experiments, in teacher effectiveness, 90–102
    implications from, 102–3
    rationale for, 90–91

Rational thought process, 89

Rationality, bounded, 88

Raudenbush, S. W., 38n107

Ray, A., 80n76

Reasoning, motivated, 88

Reliability, of classroom observation, 53, 60, 73, 75–77

Renee v. Spellings, 34n78

Research Triangle Institute, 45

Rhee, M., ix, 11

Rice, J. K., 18n1, 105n2

Rice, L. A., 19n5, 23n27, 29n53

Rich, G. A., 69n35

Richard, M., 37n92

Richardson, V., 17n22, 17n23

Richeson, J. A., 90n17

Rimm-Kaufman, S. E., 60n22

Rist, R., 38n106, 38n111

Rivers, J. C., 78n68

Rivkin, S. G., 3n18, 8n29, 19n4, 23n29, 28n47, 32n69, 32n70, 35n83, 47n152, 104n1

Robinson, M. D., 36n89

Robinson, W., 17n28, 17n30, 82n86

Rock, I., 88n5

Rockoff, J., 8n29, 20n9, 25n37, 26n38, 31n64, 47n153

Rogers, C. R., 14n11

Rogers, M. A., 71n45

Role models, passive vs. active, 35

Rosch, E., 15n15

Rose, C., 108n1

Rosenholtz, S. J., 37n97

Rosenthal, R., 36n84, 37n101, 91n18

Ross, L., 89n7

Rossi, P. H., 4n23

Rothstein, R., 32n69

Rotter, J., 37n93

Rowan, B., 29nn51–52, 31n62, 76n58, 77n59, 77nn62–63

Rubrics, performance, for quality teaching measures, 64, 65t–68t

Rushton, S., 37n92

Salaries, 3, 4, 10–11
  criteria for assigning, 104–5

Sander, W., 8n29, 23n24, 47n151

Sanders, W., 80n74, 95n24

Sanders, W. L., 8n29, 22n15, 78n68, 80n73, 82n92, 91n21

SASS (Schools and Staffing Survey), 1n3

Sass, T., 22n16, 23n28, 28n49, 29n54, 70n39, 71n44, 81n79

Schacter, J., 42n131, 64n30

Scheerens, J., 44n141

Schoenfeld, A. H., 16n21, 46n148

School administrators, teacher evaluation by, 69–71

Schools and Staffing Survey (SASS), 1n3

Schwab, R. M., 1n8

Schwerdt, G., 44n142

Scientific evidence, 39

Scoop Notebook, 75

Self-reports, teacher, 75–77

Sensitivity, teacher, as CLASS dimension, 58, 59t

Sexton, S., 82n87

Shapiro, J. M., 91n19

Shulman, L. S., 28n50

Siegel, P. M., 4n23

Siegel, R., 85–87

Siekkinen, M., 60n22

Silva, T., 27n41

Silver, E. A., 74nn52–53

Simons, D. J., 88n5

Sindelar, P. T., 13n3

Singer, J. D., 1n6, 2n14

Sireci, S. G., 54n9

Skinner, E. A., 17n25

Slater, S. C., 42n130

Sleep, L., 62n26, 62n28

Sloman, S. A., 89n11

Smith, A., 38n111

Smith, D., 49n157

Smith, J. B., 14n9

Smith, T., 6n28, 7

Snow, R. E., 38n102, 38n104, 38n107

Soar, R., 13n5

Song, J., 49n157

Southern Regional Board of Education (SREB), 45

Sparks, R., 13n5

Spitz, H. H., 38n107

Staiger, D. O., 8n29, 10n42, 20n9, 25n37, 26n38

Standardized test scores, 80

Standards
  for mathematics, 114n136
  for quality teaching measures, 64, 65t–68t

Stanovich, K. E., 89n12

Star, J. R., 74nn52–53

STAR (Student Teacher Achievement Ratio) project, 47, 116n156

Status models, value-added modeling vs., 79

Stecher, B., 75n54, 81n80

Steele, M., 42n130

Steffy, B. E., 69n33, 91n20

Sternberg, R. J., 15nn16–17

Strong, M., 87n1, 88n2

Stronge, J. H., 21n13, 22n14, 37n98, 73n49

Student(s)
  achievement of. See Student achievement
  background of, test scores and, 80
  regard for perspectives of, as CLASS dimension, 58, 59t
  surveys of teacher pedagogical practice, 45
  teacher evaluation by, 78
  and teacher interactions, 58

Student achievement
  Black-White achievement gap, 36
  pedagogical practice and, 40–46
  teacher accountability and, 105
  teacher effectiveness measured by, 46–48
  teacher ratings and, 55
Student Teacher Achievement Ratio (STAR)
    project, 47, 116n156
Study of Instructional Improvement (SII), 76
Summers, A., 23nn19–20
Support, in CLASS
  emotional, 58, 59t
  instructional, 58, 59t
Surveys, on pedagogical practice, 43–45. See
    also specific surveys by name
Swanson, E., 75n56
Swanson, M., 20n6
System 1/System 2 cognitive operations,
    89–90

Tabachnick, B. R., 14n8
Taylor, E. S., 55n15
Taylor, M. C., 38n106
Teach For America (TFA), 10n38, 24–25,
    26, 33, 104
Teacher(s)
  attributes of. See Teacher attributes
  characteristics of, 37
  identifying successful, 85–103
  qualifications of. See Teacher qualifications
  rating experiments, 90–102
Teacher attributes
  gender, 36, 82
  personal, 13–15, 36–38, 49
  race, 35–36, 82
  verbal ability, 39–40
Teacher effectiveness, 16–17, 46–48
  accountability and, 105
  certification and, 32–35
  evidence of, implications from, 104–5

measurement of, 52, 85–87, 90–103. See also
    Experiments, in teacher rating
  as student achievement measure, 46–48
  as teacher quality measure, 49
Teacher Effectiveness Rating Form, 22
Teacher evaluation, 69–75, 78, 91
  by school administrators, 69–71
  by students, 75–77
  by teacher portfolios, 72–73
  by teacher self-reports, 75–77
  by teaching artifacts, 73–75
  value-added modeling for. See Value-added
    modeling (VAM)
Teacher portfolios, 72–73
Teacher prestige, rankings for
  current vs. deserved, 5, 6t
  relative, 4, 5t
Teacher qualifications, 12–13, 18–19
  advanced degrees, 23
  content knowledge, 28–29
  evidence of, 48–50, 83–84
  pedagogical content knowledge, 28–29
  preparation program types, 24–27
  professional development, 29–30
  teacher effectiveness and, 32–35
  teaching experience, 30–32
  test scores, 28
  undergraduate courses and institution,
    22–23
  variables in, 18–19
Teacher quality, 3, 12–13
  certification and, 19–22
  decline in, 2, 2t
  definition of, 13
  effectiveness and, 16–17, 49. See also
    Teacher effectiveness
  evaluation of, 69–71
  meaning of, 12–17
  measurement of, 52–84. See also Teacher
    qualifications

(continued)

Teacher quality (continued)
  rating experiments, 90–103
  research on, 18–50. *See also* Pedagogical
      practice studies; Teacher attributes;
      Teacher effectiveness; Teacher
      qualifications
Teacher self-reports, 75–77
Teacher sensitivity, as CLASS dimension,
    58, 59t
Teacher surveys, of pedagogical practice,
    43–45
Teacher–student interactions, 58
Teaching
  demographics of, 1–3
  experience level, 30–32
  job satisfaction and, 6–7, 7t
  as occupation, 1–11. *See also* Occupation
      rankings
  policy reforms and, 7–11
  preparing for, 24–27
  salaries and, 3, 4, 10–11, 104–5
  skills and practices used in, 16, 40–41.
      See also Pedagogical practice
Teaching artifacts, 73–75
Teaching practice, 40–46
TECAT (Texas Examination of Current
    Administrators and Teachers), 28
Temin, P., 1n1
Tennessee Value Added Assessment System
    (TVAAS), 80
Test scores, 28
  value-added vs. standardized, 80
Texas Examination of Current Administrators
    and Teachers (TECAT), 28, 39
"Thin slice" experiments, 91–103
  rationale for, 90–91
Thomas, D. S., 38n109
Thomas, E., 79n70, 81n79
Thomas, W. I., 38n109
Thoreson, A., 34n77

Thought processes, 89
The Three Minute Classroom Walkthrough
    (Downey et al.), 91
Thum, Y. M., 42n131, 64n30
Tickle, L., 15n13
TIMSS (Trends in International Mathematics
    and Science Study), 44, 45, 115n144
Tom, D. Y. H., 36n86
Traditionally certified (TC) programs, 27
Treas, J., 4n25
Treiman, D., 4n23
Trends in International Mathematics and
    Science Study (TIMSS), 44, 45, 115n144
Troops to Teachers, 24
Trope, Y., 89n11
Tucker, P. D., 21n13, 22n14, 37n98, 73n49
TVAAS (Tennessee Value Added Assessment
    System), 80
Tyler, J. H., 55n15

U.S. National Academy of Engineering,
    16n18
U.S. National Academy of Sciences, 16n18
Umland, K., 62n29
U.S. Department of Education, 2n15, 35n79,
    39n114

Validity, of classroom observation, 53, 60, 73,
    75–77, 97, 103
Validity theory, 117n9
Value-added modeling (VAM), 17, 46n150,
    47, 78–84, 102, 103
  defined, 17
  key features of, 109n24
  purpose of, 46, 116n150
Value-added scores, 91
  biased, 94
  calculation of, 79–82, 120n21
  publication of, ix
  use of, 82, 121n24

Van Winkle, J., 76n57

Verbal ability, as teacher attribute, 39–40

Vigdor, J., 21n12, 23n21, 23n28, 28n48

Villegas, A. M., 35n79

Von Minden, A. M., 14n7

Vygotsky, L. S., 89n10

Wachtel, H. K., 78n66

Walker, R. J., 14n6

Walls, R. T., 14n7

Walsh, K., 26n40, 33n75

Walsh, K. C., 9n33

Ward, T. J., 21n13, 22n14, 37n98

Wason, P. C., 88n3

Wass, H. L., 14n12

Wayne, A., 18n1, 22n17, 40n122

Webb, R., 37n97

Webb, R. B., 37n97

Webster, W. J., 17n27

Wei, R. C., 82n88

Weinfeld, F. D., 9n31, 39n115

Weinstein, R. S., 38n106

Weisberg, D., 82n87

Wenglinsky, H., 22n18, 29n57

West, C., 38n107, 38n111

West, R. F., 89n12

White, B., 41n126

Whitehurst, G. J., 10n42

Whole-class instruction, 92n22

The Widget Effect (Weisberg et al.), 82, 119n88

Wilkerson, D. J., 71n45

Wilkins, R. D., 69n36

Willett, J. B., 1n6, 2n14

Wilson, S. M., 19n2

Wineburg, S. S., 38n107

Wise, A., 1n9

Witcher, A. E., 14n7

Witty, P., 13n4

Wolfes, B., 23n20

Wood, A. C., 75n54

Wooten, A. L., 55n15

Wright, P., 80n74

Wright, S. P., 22n15, 78n68, 80n77

Wuppermann, A. C., 44n142

Wyckoff, J., 26n39, 60n24, 62n25

York, R., 9n31, 39n115

Youngs, P., 18n1, 22n17, 39n117, 40n122

Zau, A., 19n5, 23n27, 29n53

Zeichner, K. M., 14n8

Zellman, G., 37n96

About the Author

Michael Strong is a senior researcher at the University of California, Santa Cruz, and at the newly formed National Laboratory of Educational Transformation. He studies teachers and teaching, and is currently working on the validation of a new observational measure of teacher evaluation called RATE (Rapid Assessment of Teacher Effectiveness). He was director of research at the New Teacher Center for 11 years and prior to that was director of research at the Center on Deafness at the University of California, San Francisco. He is a graduate of the University of London and has a doctorate in education from the University of California, Berkely.